Phuket

Front cover: secluded Laem Singh beach
on Phuket's west coast

Right: a traditional Thai boat

TOP 10 ATTRACTIONS

Khao Phra Taew National Park Waterfalls, rare flowers and gibbons make trekking here a magical experience *(page 55)*

Hat Patong Phuket's most popular beach is the place to go for all manner of water sports *(page 26)*

Wat Chalong • Soak up the culture at Phuket's most distinctive temple *(page 58)*

Island-hopping Choose a tropical paradise to the south of Phuket *(page 63)*

Phang Nga Bay Take a cruise around this bizarre seascape, scattered with towering limestone pillars *(page 68)*

Promthep Cape Arrive early if you want a good spot for the spectacular sunsets *(page 62)*

Phuket Fantasea This award-winning theme park stages elaborate shows with elephants, acrobats and lasers *(page 36)*

Phuket Town Take a walking tour around the colonial mansions and Sino-Portuguese shop-houses *(page 42)*

Orchid Garden and Thai Village Dancing, cookery, elephant training and, of course, orchids *(page 50)*

Ko Phi Phi This beautiful island is justly famous *(page 74)*

CONTENTS

68

92

51

44

Features

81

105

INTRODUCTION

At 570 sq km (220 sq miles), Phuket (pronounced 'poo-get') is known as the 'Pearl of the Andaman' due to its 49km- (30-mile-) long and 21km- (13-mile-) wide pearl-like shape, as well as its physical beauty. Phuket is Thailand's largest island, and its smallest province. It has been transformed over the past three decades from a sleepy little place into one of the country's most popular beach destinations, receiving around four million tourists each year. Sandy white beaches and crystal waters lure an escalating volume of visitors, and an increasing number of foreigners are emigrating here permanently.

Phuket's interior is mountainous, with the highest peak reaching an impressive 529m (1,735ft). Roads link the main points of interest, and although the areas surrounding the beaches are flat and easy to navigate on foot, the sheer size of the island makes transport a necessity if you intend to explore if fully. Striking headlands of varying height and length punctuate the 48km- (30-mile-) shoreline that runs down the west coast. It is here that you will find the majority of accommodation, sights and attractions. Phuket's beaches each have a unique appeal, and range from tiny, rarely visited coves whose waters teem with tropical fish, to bustling hives of action where beach activities and large numbers of people are the norm.

There are few beaches on the largely undeveloped east coast; instead this area is a haven for sailors. Yachts regularly sail around the tranquil Laem Panwa peninsula, or set sail from Laem Panwa towards the neighbouring province of Phang Nga to the north, where hundreds of pinnacles jut from perfectly still sea waters.

Longtail boats at Ko Phi Phi

Two Distinct Seasons

Phuket has two distinct seasons – dry and wet. The dry season begins in November, when skies are blue, clouds are largely absent and humidity is low. Temperatures hover around the low to mid-30s (86–95°F). March and April are still within the dry season, but both heat and humidity begin to rise in preparation for the wet season. Temperatures regularly reach the high 30s (100°F), and occasionally even creep into the 40s (110°F). Sea breezes provide relief, and virtually all buildings are air conditioned, but it is still extremely hot. Without adequate sun protection, it can take as little five minutes for skin to burn.

By May, temperatures begin to drop as the monsoon winds and rains cool the island. The rain usually starts at this time, and lasts until around November. Despite the occasional extended rainy spell, however, storms often blow in only during the late afternoons and evenings. Large periods of the 'wet'

Sunset on Patong Beach

season have been known to
see no rain at all. Daytime
temperatures between May
and November are pleasant,
usually hovering around the
mid- to high 20s (77–84°F).

Phuket's peak season is,
predictably, in the middle
of the dry season, which co-
incides with Christmas and
the New Year. The island is
always at maximum capacity
at this time, and it is advisable to book accommodation
well in advance.

A lotus flower

Flora and Fauna

Warm temperatures and jungle-filled interiors provide perfect conditions for a wide range of flora and fauna. Towering palm trees grow island-wide, and deep-purple orchids
are in such abundance that they frequently appear as deco-
rations in drinks, on hotel-room pillows and threaded to-
gether as flower garlands for sale on the streets and in bars.
Orchid farms dotted across Phuket sell flowers to take home,
and have demonstrations showing how to cultivate them.

As little as 100 years ago, a missionary named John
Carrington reported seeing tigers and elephants roaming the
island. Wild tigers are a thing of the past, but there are still
large numbers of elephants on Phuket – although they can
now only be seen inside the island's well-maintained elephant
camps. Phuket's forested interiors are still home to a few
species of wild monkeys, along with many birds and reptiles.

There are over 40 varieties of snake on the island, of which
several are poisonous. The most dangerous are those from

the pit-viper family and the notorious cobra, but snakebites are extremely rare. Snakes typically avoid populated areas, but common sense dictates that any seen should be presumed poisonous and avoided. Far more common are geckos and other small lizards, which appear mainly after dark and gather in groups around lights and neon signs in a search of an insect dinner.

Religious Beliefs

The island has a permanent population of about 300,000, of whom the majority are Theravada Buddhists. Interestingly though, Phuket has more mosques than Buddhist *wats* (temples). With their grand designs and central positioning, temples give the appearance of being greater in number. The majority of mosques are concentrated inland in the Muslim-dominated areas, which are generally less visited by the island's guests. Around 35 percent of the island's inhabitants are Muslim. It should be noted that the violence in the nearby south of Thailand has not spread to Phuket, and there is little or no religious tension between Phuket's Buddhists and Muslims.

Wat Chalong

Although smaller in number, other faiths, including Christianity – whose adherents are rapidly rising in number – and Sikhism are also recognised and readily accepted. Visitors to temples are expected to dress modestly in clothing that covers the knees and shoulders. Shoes, hats and sunglasses should be removed before entering. Some mosques allow foreign visitors, but not when ceremonies are taking place. There are a number of Christian churches across the island, and all welcome international visitors.

A young Muslim

Tourism in Paradise

By both Thai and international standards Phuket is a very rich island. There was a time when most of the island's revenue was earned from tin mining, but when tin prices began to fall, many local landowners sold their land to eager developers, making big profits in the process. Phuket emerged as a tourist destination from the late 1970s onwards, and tourism remains the leading source of income today. There are, however, a number of local residents who still maintain a more traditional lifestyle, working in the rubber and pineapple plantations.

Although mainly a beach resort, Phuket has orchid farms, forests and wild parks. Phuket Town's centre is a mixture of quaint and modern shops, newly emerging department stores, local markets and grand colonial buildings. There are viewpoints, sunset spots and temples galore, and visitors can enjoy scuba-diving, snorkelling, yachting, water-skiing, windsurfing, jet-skiing and parasailing. Boat trips on longtails, yachts, speedboats and Chinese junks run daily.

Nightlife is plentiful. Phuket Town boasts a number of entertainment establishments, and the famous Soi Bangla in Patong has clubs, pubs and bars on a scale that cannot be matched elsewhere. At the other end of the spectrum, there are intimate beach bars, hilltop jazz bars and romantic restaurants.

Activities range from jungle walks and elephant treks to bungee-jumping and horse-riding. Golfers are spoilt for choice, with four fine courses and a number of smaller greens and driving ranges. Spas, massage outlets and beauticians around the island are ready and willing to pamper. There are large shopping centres, department stores, art and antique galleries and markets.

Phuket Stands Firm

Troubled times in recent years have not affected Phuket's popularity, and if anything the international exposure it has had since the turn of the millennium has placed the island even more decisively on the map. Phuket recovered quickly from the destruction caused by the 2004 tsunami. Safety procedures and tsunami warning towers are now in place, giving visitors the reassurance of an immediate alert in the highly unlikely event of such a large-scale disaster occurring again. Threats throughout Asia of bird flu and Sudden Acute Respiratory Syndrome (Sars) did not affect Phuket, and visitors continued to flock to the island even when it hit the headlines once more in September 2007, when a plane crashed on landing at Phuket International Airport, killing 91 of the passengers on board.

A BRIEF HISTORY

Throughout the ages, Phuket has held a magnetic appeal for those who stumbled across its shores. The first inhabitants are thought to have arrived about 40,000 years ago. These hunter-gatherers inhabited an island that was almost completely covered in rainforest. They were joined in the 1st century BC by Indian settlers. The first written mention of the island was in the 2nd century AD, in the work of Claudius Ptolemy, a Greek geographer and astronomer, who published a map showing what seems to be Phuket. Early maps of Thailand (known as Siam until the early 20th century) refer to Phuket as Jang Si Lang, which was translated into English as Junk Ceylon.

An early map of Thailand

Phuket's deposits of tin attracted attention from very early times. Although no written records accurately date the initial discovery of tin, analysis of cave drawings and other artefacts suggests that it could date back as far as the Stone Age. In ancient times, rain would wash away soil to expose the underlying tin, allowing people access to it. Tin mining began much later.

Sea gypsies (*chao lay*) were early coastal inhabitants of

Phuket. They still live in small numbers in coastal communities around the island, leading a simple, mainly self-sufficient lifestyle *(see page 52)*, unlike their forebears in previous centuries, who made a living from piracy and pearl-fishing.

Phuket's Early Years

Little is known of Phuket's history until about the 16th century, when tin mining began. Not long afterwards, in the 17th and 18th centuries, European sea captains took advantage of Phuket's geographical position along the maritime trading routes between China and India. They recognised the island as a source of fresh water and firewood, and many ships would anchor in the island's bays and coves, replenishing their provisions and waiting in safety for days, weeks or even months for the northeast monsoon winds to cease before continuing safely on their passage.

Invasion by the Burmese

In 1785 Phuket came under siege during an attempted invasion by the Burmese army. Sir Francis Light, a former British East India Company captain, who had moved to the

Phuket Almost Becomes British

When the British secured a tin-mining concession in the mid-1770s, they considered Phuket as a possible base for controlling the Malacca Straits. They sent a British East India Company captain, Sir Francis Light, to reconnoitre the island, and came close to claiming Phuket as part of the British Empire. Ultimately, however, Britain opted for Penang in Malaysia instead. Captain Light fell in love and married a local island girl. His relocation to Phuket would prove significant in years to come, when he tipped off Phuket's administration that the Burmese army was going to to invade the island.

Burmese ship in a battle against the Thais

island years previously and married a local girl, witnessed the Burmese forces preparing to attack and sent word to Phuket's administration warning them of the threat. A defence was mounted by Lady Chan, the wife of Phuket's recently deceased governor, and her sister Lady Mook, who rallied the people and rapidly put forces in position to defend the island. For a month the Burmese attacked Phuket, trying to overrun it as part of a wider strategy to invade Thailand, but on 13 March they were forced to abort their invasion. The two sisters were credited with the successful defence of Phuket, and were awarded the honorary titles of Thao Thep Kasatri and Thao Sri Sunthon by Siam's King Rama I. Statues of the two sisters with swords drawn stand today on top of the Heroines' Monument in the Thalang district (see page 54 and picture on page 16).

Burmese forces invaded again during the reign of King Rama II (1809–24); this time they were successful. Islanders

Lady Chan and Lady Mook, defenders of Phuket

were forced to flee to the neighbouring province of Phang Nga, on the mainland, until the Burmese threat subsided. They returned to the northern part of Phuket and founded the town of New Thalang (since renamed Thalang), midway between where Phuket International Airport and Phuket Town now stand. Thalang was prominent until the discovery of tin in the south demanded an administrative location closer to the centre of the industry.

The Tin-Mining Era

In the early 19th century, Phuket Town in the south of the island became the administrative centre of the southern provinces of Siam, and tin production was the main source of revenue. Phuket was officially elevated to the status of a town in 1850. As Phuket's economy boomed, the demand for workers rose, and Chinese immigrants arrived in large numbers to work in the mines. Phuket still has the highest percentage of ethnic Chinese in Thailand. Another effect of tin mining was the demise of the island's hunter-gatherers, driven out of their ancestral lands by the miners.

The Miners' Rebellion

The good fortune brought to Phuket by the economic success of the tin-mining industry was not without its problems. In 1876, rivalries between two Chinese secret societies, coupled with the miners' dissatisfaction with working conditions, led to the Miners' Rebellion. Miners and police faced off in vicious battles that spilled onto the streets, until Luang Pro Chaem, a prominent monk, eventually calmed the crowds and healed the rift by acting as a mediator between the opposing parties. Luang Pro Chaem set and healed many of the broken bones and wounds that resulted from the battles. A statue paying tribute to him and the good deeds he did for the people of Phuket can be seen at the famous Wat Chalong temple.

The Colonial Period

As the economy prospered, some of the Chinese immigrants became wealthy mineowners. During the 19th century, the face of Phuket Town steadily began to change, to reflect the culture of the now dominant Chinese and the influence of Europeans. Grand mansions and shop-houses were built in the distinctive Sino-Portuguese style *(see page 42)*, which the Chinese borrowed from British colonies in Singapore and what is now Malaysia, where the Portuguese had had an early influence on building design. Many of these buildings still stand today in the older quarters of Phuket

Chinese-influenced temple design, Phuket Town

Town, having been renovated and transformed into cafés, art galleries and museums.

The Rubber Industry

Henry Nicholas Ridley, a botanist at the Singapore Botanical Garden, discovered the full potential of the rubber tree in 1888 when he devised a way to propagate the trees swiftly and tap them for their sap, using a method that is essentially the same today. A small cup collects the latex flowing from a cut in a tree, stretching one-third to one-half of the tree's circumference, after which the original cut is shaved thin and the tree is re-tapped. The bark is given a chance to renew itself once the cuttings reach the ground, during which a new tapping panel is started elsewhere on the tree.

Phuket's first rubber tree arrived in 1903, and soon the trees began appearing in straight lines across the landscape

The ordered rows of a rubber plantation

– more than one-third of the island is now covered with plantations. As with the tin-mining industry, rubber-tapping called for a new wave of immigrants to meet the rising workload. This time it was not the Chinese, but Muslims from what is now Malaysia who arrived in droves. Thai Muslims still account for the majority of those working in Phuket's rubber plantations.

Rubber-tapping

Rubber export was extremely lucrative, but over the years demand for natural latex went through a series of ups and downs. Aircraft and automobile manufacturers required rubber in large quantities to make tyres, but when the cost of synthetic rubber came down after the 1940s, the demand for natural latex decreased. The industry spiralled downwards and many rubber plantations were abandoned. However, the mid-1980s saw a dramatic and sudden turn-around when the worldwide Aids epidemic created a huge demand for natural latex to manufacture condoms and surgical gloves. Most of Phuket's rubber plantations were gradually brought back into production and are once again busy. They are continually being upgraded with higher-yielding trees.

The Modernisation of Phuket

At the beginning of the 20th century, a huge fire ravaged most of the downtown area of Phuket Town. The town was subsequently rebuilt, transforming it into a modern city. Governor Rassada Korsimbi led the reconstruction effort, and Rassada Road was named in his honour.

Tourism came to the island in the 1970s, when the rubber industry was in a slump and there were no more profits to be made from tin mining. But there were formidable obstacles to be overcome before mass tourism could become viable. Despite its relatively large size, Phuket was at that time fairly isolated. The few roads were primitive, and during the monsoon season virtually impassable. The only way to reach Phuket was by boat until Phuket International Airport was constructed in 1972. At the same time, a major road-building project commenced, and the first tourist accommodation appeared in the form of a few basic bungalows on Patong Beach, which at the time was all but deserted. Backpackers were the first to discover the island's pristine beaches.

Phuket experienced an almost overnight transition from an industrial- to a tourism-driven economy. The island's popularity among foreign visitors skyrocketed, and in the 1980s and 1990s Phuket saw a spurt of resort-building to cope with the demand. The new millennium, however, brought with it many challenges. In 2002 Sudden Acute Respiratory Syndrome (Sars) spread throughout Asia, threatening to affect the tourism industry. Thankfully, Phuket escaped lightly, as did Thailand as a whole, where there were only eight suspected cases. The following year the number of visitors to Phuket actually increased, despite the Avian flu epidemic.

But catastrophe struck in 2004. The deadly tsunami that invaded Phuket's shores on 26 December of that year was triggered by an undersea earthquake in the Indian Ocean off the west coast of Sumatra at 7.58am local time. A series of waves crashed onto the western coast over the coming hours, with a force that has since been compared by scientists to that of a 747 aircraft travelling at full speed. In Thailand, the official death total was 5,395, with a further 2,845 listed as missing.

On Phuket, an estimated 320 people were killed, although unofficially many more are thought to have died because of the vast numbers of illegal workers on the island (many of them from Burma). The true death toll may never be known. Kamala was one of the worst-hit beaches, but Patong was also very badly affected. Tributes to the dead are held annually across the island, and life-saving measures have

Memorial to the 2004 tsunami on Patong Beach

A bright future awaits

been put into place in the unlikely event of such a disaster reoccurring. Warning towers are positioned along all beaches to sound the alarm, and signs show the way to safe evacuation areas inland. A 12-month period of rebuilding and recovery followed the tsunami, and by late 2005 Phuket was once again thriving.

Around this time, violence in Thailand's southern provinces of Narathiwat, Pattani, Songkhla and Yala failed to reach the island, and the political rallies against ousted prime minister Thaksin Shinawatra were confined to the capital, Bangkok. Phuket seemed finally to have entered a period of ease until 17 September 2007, when a plane from Bangkok crashed on landing during severe weather at Phuket International Airport. Ninety-one passengers were killed.

Despite these recent natural and man-made disasters, the popularity of Phuket with foreign visitors has not declined. And no wonder. It remains a beautiful island, diverse in its attractions, and is still an inexpensive destination. With each passing year visitor numbers increase, bringing with them more revenue, which in turn leads to further development. As further flight routes are established, even more people will be able to visit the island. The rich and famous frequent Phuket more than any other island in Thailand, and with approximately four million tourists visiting each year, Phuket is firmly established as one of the most popular holiday destinations in Southeast Asia.

Historical Landmarks

1st century BC Southeast Indian colonists land in Phuket.

17th century European sailors identify Phuket. Pirates plague Phuket's shores, attacking ships and stealing slaves from villages.

18th century European ships regularly call at Phuket to obtain commodities and ride out storms.

1785 Ladies Chan and Mook lead a successful defence against an attempted invasion by the Burmese.

1809–24 The Burmese attack again, driving islanders to nearby Phang Nga for a number of years.

1850 Phuket is elevated to town status.

1851–68 Phuket emerges as a leader in the tin-mining industry.

1876 Fights break out during a rebellion of tin miners.

c.1900 A huge fire destroys most of central Phuket Town.

1900–20 Governor Rasada Korsimbi reconstructs Phuket Town, turning it into a modern city.

1903 The first rubber tree arrives.

1916 Phuket officially becomes a province.

1970s Phuket moves away from mining and towards tourism.

mid-1980s Phuket's rubber industry takes off again.

1997 The Thai baht is devalued. Thailand enters a three-year recession.

1999–2000 The economy shows signs of recovery.

2001 Thaksin Shinawatra is elected prime minister.

2004 Attacks in Muslim provinces south of Phuket result in the deaths of more than 320 people. A tsunami strikes Phuket and much of Southeast Asia, casuing many deaths and much devastation.

2005 Prime Minister Thaksin Shinawatra's Thai Rak Thai party wins a landslide victory in the general elections.

2005–6 Phuket, and other affected parts of the country, recover from the effects of the tsunami.

2006 The Royal Thai Army stages a bloodless coup. Thaksin is unseated and a temporary military government installed.

2007 A plane from Bangkok crashes on landing at Phuket.

WHERE TO GO

The island of Phuket is located 850km (530 miles) south of Bangkok, just off the long arm of Thai territory that stretches down the Malay Peninsula. It covers an area of about 540 sq km (210 sq miles). Phuket International Airport is in the north of the island, about 30 minutes by car from the main beaches, which are dotted along the west coast. Hat Patong is the most popular beach resort, the place to head to if you are looking for action. Most of the island's accommodation, as well as restaurants, bars and shops, are located there, although nearby Kata and Karon beaches are also gaining in popularity. The capital, Phuket Town, is due east of Patong.

The northwest and south coasts of the island are favoured by those looking for a quiet holiday. Some of the most attractive beaches are found here. Most accommodation is resort-style, and there are few other facilities. The east coast has little in the way of beaches, but sailors love it, and there are a couple of luxurious marinas.

Transport around the island is mainly by tuk-tuks, which can be found in numbers around the beaches, town centres and main points of interest. Fares are negotiable. Alternatively, car and motorcycle hire is easily arranged through hotels and independent tour companies.

Phuket is surrounded by a number of small, offshore islands that are easily reached by boat from Chalong or Rawai on the south coast. Further afield, Ko Phi Phi, famous as the location of the movie *The Beach*, is only a few hours' boat ride from Rassada Pier in Phuket Town.

A visit to Phang Nga province on the mainland to the north makes an excellent day trip. From there you can kayak

Colonial architecture in Phuket Town

around the limestone pinnacles of Phang Nga Bay, or tour the intriguingly named James Bond Island. The small seaside resort of Khao Lak is a few hours north of Phuket International Airport. It is the easiest access point for the Similan Islands, which offer some of the world's best diving.

Krabi province is around three hours east of Phuket by boat. The main attractions here are a beach and an island, Ao Nang and Ko Lanta. Both could theoretically be reached in a day, although visits of two days or longer are advisable.

PATONG, KARON AND KATA

Phuket's three main beaches are Hat Patong, Hat Karon and Hat Kata. Undoubtedly the most famous of the three, and the hub of the island's activity, is the bold and brash **Hat Patong**. Love it or hate it, Patong has an undeniable pull. Accommodation ranges from budget hotels through to hillside villas – although the backpacker-type accommodation

Indian Ocean Tsunami

Phuket was hit hard by the devastating tsunami resulting from a powerful earthquake whose epicentre was off the coast of Sumatra, Indonesia, on 26 December 2004. A series of waves travelled across the Indian Ocean, reaching heights of up to 30m (98ft) around Southeast Asia. The largest wave to hit Phuket was estimated to be around 15m (49ft) high. Most of the damage in Phuket was confined to the areas around Hat Patong and Hat Kamala, with Khao Lak and Ko Phi Phi also badly affected. About 320 people are thought to have died on the island.

The government has put in place measures designed to prevent such a loss if a similar scale disaster were to occur in the future. Warning towers are set up along the beaches to sound the alarm, and routes leading to safe inland areas are well marked.

Hat Patong is Phuket's busiest beach

found elsewhere in Thailand is less common here. In comparison to popular European beach resorts, Hat Patong is not overly crowded, but it does attract larger numbers of visitors compared to other beaches on the island.

This is the most developed beach on the island. There are rows of beach umbrellas, loud noise from jet skis and numerous touts selling everything from hats to hammocks. The 2004 tsunami briefly highlighted the beach's natural beauty by clearing the sands of everything man-made for the first time in well over two decades. But today, this 3km (2-mile) stretch of sand is once again littered with people and parasols.

If you are looking for fun rather than relaxation, Hat Patong is the place to be. Its clear waters are great for swimming and snorkelling, and there are banana boats, jet skis and parasailing to keep you occupied. Along the beach road are shops, bars and restaurants, and Patong itself is almost like

Soi Bangla by night

a mini-town but without any of the cultural attractions. Rainy days can be spent bowling, shopping, bungee-jumping or seeing a show.

Slightly north of Patong Beach is the much smaller **Kalim Bay**, which is usually simply regarded as an extension of Patong, despite officially being a separate area. Although it is fairly rocky and is not recommended for swimming because of its choppy waves, this small strip is picturesque, especially when viewed from above. A few high-class restaurants, including Phuket's most famous dining establishment, Baan Rim Pa *(see page 137)*, are located above the bay.

Soi Bangla (Bangla Road)

Many visitors to Hat Patong make at least one night-time visit to the notorious **Soi Bangla**. The action-packed street is a frenzy of bars, pubs, clubs, restaurants and street stalls, with the odd tailor thrown in for good measure. The street is open to traffic throughout the day but becomes pedestrian-only at night, making it a lot easier – and safer – to stumble down. The mainly open-air bars at the beach end of the road are fairly cheap and cheerful, and are popular with sex tourists. The bar girls are usually very friendly, and virtually all are for sale, so do not be surprised to see them disappearing with customers throughout the night. The sex trade, which has a somewhat less sordid image in Thailand than in the Western world, is rife in the country's principal tourist destinations.

The further from the beach you walk, the louder and more intense the activity seems to get. In the centre of Soi Bangla are a number of *katoey* bars, where men dress nightly in elaborate cabaret-type outfits, complete with feather headpieces and chiselled make-up. Nightclubs are mostly found at the top of the road, and are mainly located above huge entertainment complexes. **Patong Boxing Stadium**, at the far end of Soi Bangla, holds Muay Thai kickboxing fights between Thais and foreigners at 8pm every Monday, Thursday and Saturday.

Patong's Other Attractions

Many of Hat Patong's visitors are unaware that just around the corner is a much quieter and more peaceful beach. As the one track to this beach is over private land, the only way to reach it is by boat. **Freedom Beach**, as it is known to locals, is a 15-minute hop away from Hat Patong's southern end.

Patong Beach

There is no accommodation on the beach, but there is a seating area in front of a row of coconut palms, and a few small restaurants. Rocks and coral close to shore at the southern corner make for some excellent snorkelling opportunities.

At the southern end of Hat Patong is **Simon Cabaret** (daily, show times 7.30pm and 9.30pm; charge; tel: 0 7634 2011; www.phuket-simoncabaret.com), an entertainment complex offering Las Vegas-style shows featuring Thailand's infamous lady boys. The shows are popular but a bit tacky, with the performing *katoey* obviously miming words, overacting horrendously and dancing in a ridiculously overchoreographed manner. Even so, the sight of so many men looking deceptively feminine draws curious crowds night after night. You can have your photo taken with the cast afterwards; expect to pay for the privilege.

Patong is a great place to shop. Stalls line the beachside and Soi Bangla. Similar products can often be found at a cheaper price in Phuket Town, although Patong usually has a greater selection. Expect to see lots of custom-made jewellery, fake designer clothes and handbags, and pirated DVDs. Phuket's largest shopping centre, **Jungceylon** (www.jungceylon.com), opened in 2007 on Rat Utit Road. It contains a large number of shops, as well as restaurants, bars, a cinema and accommodation. Art-lovers should make a trip to **Phrachanukhro Road**, where a number of galleries are located alongside each other, and paintings can be purchased or produced to your own requirements.

Dream home?

Phuket's property market is booming thanks to an increasing number of expatriate buyers. Dream homes sell at a fraction of what they would cost in Europe, but property laws and ownership regulations for foreign investors change frequently, making a reputable lawyer a must.

Hat Karon

Hat Karon

To the south of Hat Patong is **Hat Karon**, a 10-minute scenic drive over a coastal hill from its more famous neighbour. This banana-shaped beach has the advantage of being somewhat less chaotic than Hat Patong, while still being close to all the action. At 4km (2½ miles) in length, it is slightly longer than Hat Patong, and with little development near its golden shores, it has a much more natural feel to it. A grassy embankment lined with trees separates it from the surrounding road and hotels. While Hat Patong is more of a bay, which is broken up with a few islands in the distance, Hat Karon is a long, windswept beach with a strong sea breeze and often crashing waves. Red flags are common across the whole island during the monsoon season (May to late October), and Hat Karon in particular seems to be more blustery than a lot of the other beaches. Hat Karon does not offer the water sports that Patong or

Kata beaches do, but the waves during the rainy season are fantastic for surfers. Snorkelling is excellent around a coral reef to the southern headland which separates Hat Karon from Hat Kata.

There are a number of shops, and a few bars and restaurants around Hat Karon. Most distinctive is **Dino Park** (daily 10am–10pm; charge; tel: 0 7633 0625; www.dino park.com), a dining and mini-golf complex. Golfers weave through prehistoric landscapes, crossing over bridges and lakes and passing large models of dinosaurs with smoking nostrils. Staff at the restaurant and at the adjoining streetside bar wear Flintstones costumes, and an elephant often makes an appearance, stopping with those who are having a drink and watching the world pass by.

Enjoying the sun and surf on Hat Kata Yai

Hat Kata Yai and Hat Kata Noi

Although rapid development is beginning to change the quiet and intimate image of **Hat Kata**, it is still arguably the most scenic of Phuket's three principal beaches. Hat Kata has the best of both worlds. Its smaller size and fewer hotels give it a more relaxed feel, but there are a far greater choice of shops, bars and restaurants than Hat Karon has to offer. Those wanting some nightlife are advised to go to Hat Patong, the only place to remain a hive of activity after midnight. There are actually two Kata beaches, Hat Kata Yai (*yai* means big), commonly referred to as Kata, and Hat Kata Noi (*noi* means small). Hat Kata Yai is the busier location, where virtually all the ac-

commodation and entertainment are found. The beach itself has fine white sand and clear waters with a hue that changes from deep to light blue throughout the seasons. Some excellent snorkelling can be enjoyed around the headlands to both the north and south.

Hat Kata is quiet and romantic in the evening, with twinkling lights illuminating the strip of beach heading to the north. There is a casual reggae-type beach bar to the far south, where chunky wooden tables extend over the sea and free barbecues are held each Friday before mesmerising fire shows are staged on the sand.

To the south of the headland, **Hat Kata Noi** is much quieter than its neighbour. Under Thai law, no beach can be privately owned, but the Katathani Resort owns all of the land directly facing this beach, which means that in practical terms it is usually only the guests of the hotel who use the beach. Hat Kata Noi is similar in appearance to 'big' Kata, with white sand and calm, clear waters.

Kata Hill

Phuket has many viewpoints overlooking the beaches, mountains and Andaman Sea. A number of the more popular ones are located around Hat Kata. Seen on many

The view from Three Beaches Viewpoint

a postcard is **Three Beaches Viewpoint**, a stunning spot so named for its unique location looking down onto the headlands of Patong, Karon and Kata beaches. Due to the elevated hillside location, clouds tend to build rapidly from lunchtime onwards, so for the best views and photographs of this trio of beaches arrive early in the morning or early in the evening (in time for sunset). The viewpoint is at the peak of Kata Hill, just south of Hat Kata, and is known by all taxi and tuk-tuk drivers.

Kata boasts a number of spectacular places from which to see the sun set into the sea. The After Beach Bar is a wooden reggae bar jutting out over Kata Hill which offers cheap beer, Thai food and a chilled-out atmosphere that is perfect for enjoying the setting sun. A little further along on the opposite side of the road is **Koh Chang Elephant Camp**. Visitors can arrange to go on elephant treks, or just feed the elephants and stop for a drink at the bamboo bar at the front of the park, where they will often be joined by two resident monkeys. For something a little more upmarket, visit Ratri Jazztaurant (www.ratrijazztaurant.com), perched high in the hills off Patak Road. Cocktails are the name of the game, and live jazz features nightly. A long walk uphill is required to experience the view, but the golden orb of the sun melting into the horizon over the Andaman Sea is a stunning reward for those who do make the climb.

NORTHWEST COAST

As a general rule, the further north you go, the quieter it gets. The busy area around Hat Patong stands in stark contrast to the undeveloped beaches around the island's northern tip, which generally appeal more to those seeking a quiet, relaxing break. Although there are a few mid-range options, accommodation on the northwest coast is generally resort-based, and usually within the higher price bracket. Outside the resorts, there are far fewer restaurant and shopping facilities than there are around the main beaches, and although those within the resorts themselves are typically of a high quality, the prices reflect this. But if your budget and tastes run to it, this quieter side of Phuket is well worth experiencing – a place where beaches are less crowded, noise is kept to a minimum, and a busy day involves little other than flipping from your front to your back to ensure an even tan.

Hat Kamala, Hat Surin and Hat Bang Tao

Hat Patong's closest northerly neighbours, which are steadily increasing in popularity, are Hat Kamala and Hat Surin. Although not as quiet as the beaches to the far north, they are nowhere near as busy as Hat Patong. **Hat Kamala**, only a short hill ride away from Hat Patong, is totally different in character from its busy neighbour. Those who stay there will be blessed with a small yet pristine beach that is quiet, peaceful and well located if they should wish to venture over the hill for a bit of nightlife. The 2004 tsunami devastated Kamala, more so in fact than Patong, despite Hat Patong receiving most of the media attention, but within 12 months it was completely restored, with a make-over that gave it an even fresher, cleaner feel.

The stretch of sea-facing land above Kamala is known by locals and foreign investors as 'millionaires' mile'. Expansive villas with picture-perfect views, most worth US$1 million and above, have been carved into the hillsides to accommodate the needs of the wealthy.

Hat Kamala is the site of **Phuket Fantasea** (daily Fri–Wed 5.30–11.30pm, show time 9pm; tel: 0 7638 5333; www. phuket-fantasea.com), a self-proclaimed night-time cultural

Making friends at Phuket Fantasea

theme park located at the
foot of the hill dividing
Kamala from Surin, on the
Kamala side. A winner of the
Thailand Tourism Award
for Best Attraction, the complex hosts 'cirque du soleil'-
type acrobatic performances
and animal shows, one of
which features a stage full of
wild elephants.

With its golden rather
than white sands, **Hat Surin**

Surin is home to many Muslims

looks different from many of Phuket's other beaches. It is
nonetheless a very scenic beach, with rows of casuarina
trees to the rear and, of course, a huge expanse of sea at
the front. Hat Surin can get pretty busy at peak times, but
during the low season it is often deserted. At certain times
of year there is a strong undertow, making it more important than ever to pay attention to the red flags that indicate
potentially unsafe swimming conditions. A number of
seafood restaurants are in competition in the area, and
lunchtime offers the opportunity to sample fresh fish and
seafood at shaded bamboo tables along one of the many
beachfront outlets.

Another attraction in the area is **Laem Singh**, a tiny bay
dominated by rocks between Hat Kamala and Hat Surin. On
Sundays many people gather to eat seafood and listen to
music being played on the sand.

Both the Surin and Kamala areas are home to a high concentration of Thai Muslims, and there is therefore a more reserved atmosphere in these places. Topless sunbathing, which
is not favoured by Buddhist Thais, is even more frowned upon
here. Likewise, there are fewer late-night bars and restaurants

here than elsewhere on Phuket. Many of Phuket's mosques are found inland in the villages around Surin and Kamala.

Heading north, just a few kilometres before the next major beach of Hat Bang Tao is the much smaller **Ao Pansea**. This tiny gem of a bay is rarely visited, as it is only accessible via Phuket's most exclusive resort, the **Amanpuri** *(see page 133)*. Private residences at the resort are frequented largely by the rich and famous, who are undeterred by the extravagant price tag and lured by the guarantee of seclusion. Movie stars, rock stars and royalty have all vacationed in the private pavilions of the Amanpuri, and security guards do not hesitate to forcefully turn away unwanted visitors.

Phuket's northwest coast is the location for a number of the island's most exclusive hotels and resorts. The renowned **Laguna Phuket** complex, which consists of five luxury hotels sharing a spa, 18-hole golf course and other leisure facilities, all facing **Hat Bang Tao.** There is little development on this 8km- (5-mile-) long beach aside from Laguna Phuket, so a short stroll can lead to a virtually deserted patch of sand. Generally, the further south you walk, the quieter it becomes.

The **Phuket Laguna Riding School** (tel: 0 7632 4199), in business since 1989, has 65 horses suited to all ages and levels of riding experience. There is a choice of trekking routes, most passing through the forests and lagoons around the Laguna Phuket complex. Some treks feature rides along the sands of Hat Bang Tao.

The town of **Cherngtalay**, a few kilometres east of Hat Bang Tao, has a number of shops, bars and restaurants. Prices are a fraction of the those charged by the Laguna hotels. Just outside the town, near the Laguna complex, is the famous **Hideaway Day Spa** (tel: 0 7627 1549), which specialises in Thai massage and pampers clients on open-air Thai *salas* overlooking a peaceful freshwater lake.

The deserted sands of Hat Mai Khao

Sirinat National Park

Phuket's northwest cape is encompassed by **Sirinat National Park**, a 90-sq km- (35-sq mile-) area that takes in the beaches of Hat Mai Khao, Hat Nai Yang and Hat Nai Ton. Around three-quarters of the park is marine, extending 5km (3 miles) out to sea, with the rest made up of the adjoining beaches and mangrove forests, in which casuarina trees provide shelter for a diversity of birds, mammals and insects. Sirinat National Park is home to some of Phuket's most beautiful coral reefs, where plate and tree corals share the waters with sea fans, sea anemones and masses of brightly coloured tropical fish. The **Thachatchai Nature Trail** leading to the park's northern end follows a 600m (1,970ft) long raised wooden walkway. Along the way, signs highlight flora and fauna common to the region.

By far the smallest of the Sirinat National Park beaches is the beautiful but isolated **Hat Nai Ton**. It can be ex-

Water buffalo and egrets in the Sirinat National Park

tremely difficult to find, as it is located at the foot of a series of steep hills that require navigation through winding roads, jungle and rubber plantations. Peaceful and quiet, Hat Nai Ton offers sunbathers a tranquil spot in which to relax. Snorkelling conditions are excellent, with rocky headlands sheltered from wind and strong currents attracting marine life year-round. A wrecked tin dredger lies abandoned in the waters at a depth of 16m (52ft), to which visits can be organised through the Nai Ton Beach Resort.

Hat Nai Yang lies at the centre of this trio of beaches and is almost deserted in the monsoon season, due to its rugged and blustery appearance during this time. The wind and rain, however, take with them the leaves and branches that litter the shores following fierce storms, and by the time high season rolls around, unprepossessing Hat Nai Yang is transformed into a beauty. This lovely curving bay is the location of the headquarters of Sirinat National Park, and although not nearly as busy as the southwest coast, it is the most popular beach in this area. As there are no hotels directly on the beach itself, Hat Nai Yang manages to maintain an unspoilt feel. During high season, a row of thatched beach huts offering cold refreshments and freshly cooked seafood line the sand under the shade of evergreen trees. Snorkelling and scuba-diving trips can be arranged to a large coral reef about 1km (½ mile) out to sea, and the occasional nesting turtle will sometimes wander ashore from the neighbouring Hat Mai Khao.

Phuket's most northerly beach is also its longest. **Hat Mai Khao** is more than 17km (10½ miles) in length, yet it is one of the quietest and least developed. Only one resort, the JW Marriott Resort and Spa *(see page 134)*, stands unobtrusively on its shores. Hat Mai Khao is undoubtedly one of the most beautiful beaches on the island, with huge stretches of almost deserted powder-white sand lapped by some of the clearest turquoise waters in Phuket. Its isolated position, away from the rest of the island's accommodation and facilities, protects it from overdevelopment, as few visit the area other than those in search of seclusion.

Sea Turtle Conservation

Hat Mai Khao is home to the Marine Turtle Foundation, which was launched in 2002 to raise funds to help protect the turtles that use Hat Mai Khao as their annual nesting ground. The foundation strives to keep the area free from development to ensure the safe return of the hundreds of olive Ridley sea turtles and endangered giant leatherbacks.

Both species come back to the quiet shores where they were born to lay their eggs between November and February each year. If you are here at the right time, you can witness the thousands of hatchlings making their dash across the sand to the sea. The number of eggs laid each year is recorded by local Mai Khao villagers, who patrol the beach during the evenings to guard the nesting sites. A number of eggs are taken to a hatchery to ensure their survival in case of human or natural disturbance of the nests, and the baby turtles are released during a special ceremony in April each year.

Chinpracha House on Krabi Road

PHUKET TOWN

Although it is by no means as popular as the coastal areas, **Phuket Town** offers an eclectic mix of historic buildings, bustling markets and chic restaurants, and is steadily beginning to appeal to more visitors as a destination in its own right. Popular sights include the post-war mansions constructed by rich rubber barons and the stately Sino-Portuguese buildings built for successful tycoons during the 19th-century tin-mining era. The town has a one-way system that can be difficult to navigate by car. Most of the town works on a grid system, which makes it pretty easy to explore on foot.

Colonial Architecture

Some of Phuket's finest architecture can be seen in the **Old Town** area around Thalang, Dibuk and Krabi Roads. A number of huge colonial-style mansions, Sino-Portuguese shop-houses, and a scattering of other architecturally unique buildings were erected in this area during the 19th-century tin-mining boom, and are well preserved.

Many of the rich Chinese immigrants who amassed their wealth from the mines built mansions for themselves and their families as a display of their prominence and success. These mansions had huge entrances, terraced upper levels and elegant central courtyards. The greater the wealth, the greater the scale of design, and it was not uncommon for some of the most indulgent mansions to have two or even three courtyards.

Commonly regarded as Phuket's most beautiful home, **Phra Pitak Chinpracha Mansion** on Krabi Road was named after its owner Tan Ma Siang, who was more commonly known as Phrapitak Chinpracha. The mansion is still privately owned, and therefore not accessible to the public, but it is still worth a visit if only to admire it from the outside. To get an idea of what the interiors of these mansions look like, head next door to **Chinpracha House**, also built by Tan Ma Siang, which is open to the public for tours (Mon–Sat 9am–4.30pm, tel: 0 7621 1167).

The vast majority of Phuket's Sino-Portuguese shop-houses are on **Thalang Road**, where buildings date back between 60 and 100 years. The traditional and historical values of these buildings spared them from being torn down when Phuket began modernising, and despite being extensively renovated, the original structures still stand. Many shop-houses built during the tin-mining era have been restored into art galleries, coffee shops

Shop-houses

Phuket Town's Sino-Portuguese shop-houses are all alike in design. They are only 5m (16ft) in width but can stretch back as far as 50m (160ft). The front of each building has a sheltered entrance, and each row is usually divided into five shop houses.

Shop-house doorway

and outlets for traditional Chinese herbal medicines. Chinese lettering still appears above many doors, and the pavements are lined with grand arches divided into sections by tall Corinthian-style pillars.

Formerly the residence of tin-mining and financial agent Tan Ma Siang, number 20 Thalang Road has been restored and is now the popular **China Inn**, a colourful and artistic antiques store, restaurant and garden café decorated in rich Chinese red and gold. A few doors down is the **Phuket Art Gallery**, which is the town's first artist studio. Number 63 Thalang Road is an abandoned shop-house that is being renovated and transformed by the City Hall into a small educational museum.

Inside the elegant **Phuket Provincial Hall** on Damrong Road is an antiquated courtroom featuring a wooden judge's bench that has been in use for the past century. The Provincial Hall itself, which is just across the lawn, was made famous when it served as the French Embassy in Cambodia in the 1984 film *The Killing Fields*.

Markets and Shops

Phuket Town is *the* place to find the cheapest prices at the local markets. For clothes and accessories, the undercover

EXPO Market on Tilok Utit 2 Road changes its stock regularly, and usually has something a little different from the markets around the beaches.

Phuket's oldest and largest fresh produce market is on Ranong Road and is bustling throughout the day. The early morning is particularly busy, with locals arriving to select fruit, vegetables, herbs, spices, meat, fish and a host of other ingredients for restaurant and domestic kitchens. Most Thai cookery courses in Phuket will begin with an early morning visit to this colourful market, which was once frequented by pirates and traders.

One of Phuket's most interesting markets is also one that few seem to discover. **Talad Tai Rot**, more commonly known as the weekend market (Sat–Sun, evenings only), is located just outside Phuket Town. Two roads, Chao Fa East and Chao Fa West, head to the south of the island, and the market is on a road running between them, indicated by a road sign simply stating 'short-cut to town'. The market, opposite Wat Nakha, sells everything from clothing and accessories to household items and pets.

The Vegetarian Festival

For one week each year during the ninth lunar month, Phuket Town takes on an intensely freakish vibe as devotees take part in sunrise initiation rituals in the temple grounds to prepare to offer their bodies as living sacrifices to the gods. Entering trances, they spear their faces with anything ranging from blunt palm leaves to 2.5m (8ft) steel poles, then pace the streets as they continue to mutilate themselves with gruesome piercings, slicing their tongues and thrashing their bare backs with axes and machetes. These acts are undeniably mesmerising, but as they become more extreme each year, some have begun to question the precise nature of spiritual worship that enables or requires them.

Central Festival (daily 11am–10pm) is a large shopping complex on the outskirts of Phuket Town. It is too far from the town or beaches to walk there, so is best reached by taxi (all the drivers know where it is located), a journey of around five minutes from the town centre and 15 minutes from Hat Patong. As well as independent stalls, global franchises, a supermarket and a department store spanning four levels, Central Festival has numerous restaurants, a cinema and a spa.

The independently owned boutique within Siam Indigo Exotique Bar and Restaurant on Phang Nga Road is more intimate, and features a stunning collection of clothing, jewellery and accessories.

Phuket Town Temples

There are temples all over the island of Phuket. The best-known is in the Chalong area, aptly named Wat Chalong, but most are located in and around Phuket Town. Each is unique and often has a history steeped in legend and folk-lore. Due to a strong Chinese influence resulting from the influx of immigrants during the 19th century, many of Phuket Town's temples are Taoist.

Figurine in Jui Tui temple

The oldest Chinese temple is **Put Jaw**, on Ranong Road near the town centre. Built over two centuries ago, and dedicated to Kwan Im, the Chinese goddess of mercy, it suffered severe damage in a fire and was renovated around 100 years ago. Although not the island's most architecturally impressive temple, Put Jaw is nevertheless one of the

Put Jaw Chinese temple

more interesting to visit. An image of Kwan Im stands in the middle hall, surrounded by numerous fortune-telling devices. The simplest of these divining methods involves a pair of red wooden blocks – the idea is to ask a question and let the blocks fall to the floor in front of an altar. A 'yes' or 'no' answer is determined according to which way they land. Alternatively, the 'can and stick' method of divinity requires a bit more effort. Two cans filled with numbered sticks are vigorously shaken until one of the sticks falls out. The numbered stick is then taken to a room filled with boxes containing corresponding numbered slips, to which the advice written should be the answer to the question you asked. Paper slips are in Thai, so you may need an interpreter, but a few people around the temple grounds speak English.

Adjoining Put Jaw is the much more visually spectacular **Jui Tui** temple, dedicated to Kiu Wong, the Chinese vegetarian god who is worshipped annually during the week-long Vegetarian Festival, when hundreds invoke spirits to enable them to perform extreme acts of self-mutilation in dedication to the gods. Huge teak doors depicting carvings of guardians lead into the temple, where a red-faced statue of Kiu Wong sits on an altar surrounded by offerings of various fruits and vegetables. Although dramatic and somewhat creepy-looking, the red-faced statue is intended to indicate benevolence and not fierceness or aggression.

Erected in 1853, **Sanjao Sam San**, on Krabi Road, is a more peaceful temple, dedicated to Tien San Sung Moo, the goddess of the sea and the patron saint of sailors. Sanjao Sam San has a much more refined ambience, with gold statues of two lions on the outside and intricate carvings displayed on the inner walls. Ceremonies are traditionally held in the temple grounds to bless the launch of new boats and to ask for the sailors' safety and protection.

Parks and Viewpoints

A public park at **Saphan Hin**, located in Phuket Town where Phuket Road meets the sea, is popular with joggers, who take advantage of the mangrove- and tree-lined trails that wind around it. The park also has a fitness centre, stadium, restaurants and food stalls. Muay Thai kickboxing fights are held in the stadium each Friday evening, and a number of festivals and events take place within the park grounds throughout the year. Slightly out of the

The Buddha statue at Khao Rang

The view from Khao Rang

town itself is **King Rama IX Park,** which is more commonly known as **Suan Luang.** Although not as large as Saphan Hin, Suan Luang is also popular with exercisers. Many people arrive in the early mornings to participate in t'ai chi lessons, or to jog around the tree-lined lotus ponds.

Khao Rang is Phuket Town's only real viewpoint, from which panoramas of the southern part of the island can be enjoyed. The hill also receives cooling breezes. Tung-Ka Café *(see page 141)* sits near the peak of the hill and is open throughout the day, serving Thai food to patrons watching the bustling town below. Bordered by frangipani and bougainvillea, and bordered by forest to the sides and above, the area attracts birds during the day and choruses of crickets in the evenings. This can be a great place to watch the evening sun setting over the town. A huge 9m (29ft) Buddha statue in the 'suppression evil' pose is located about halfway up Khao Rang on the northern side.

In the Orchid Garden

Northern Outskirts

The **Orchid Garden and Thai Village** (daily 8am–9pm; charge; tel: 0 7623 7400) is a large cultural centre offering Thai dancing and shows, handmade crafts, traditional Thai restaurants and elephant training. This is also the location for glitzy wedding services, with ceremonies steeped in Thai culture and tradition; the bride and groom can even arrive on elephant-back – a Thai alternative to a horse and carriage.

Butterfly Garden and Insect World (daily 9am–5.30pm; charge; tel: 0 7621 5616). Featuring more than 40 species of butterfly in a natural rainforest environment, this is a peaceful place to spend a few hours. Also on display are large spiders, stick insects and scorpions. A separate enclosure houses rare and native birds of Thailand. Factual displays give details about the species and their natural habitats.

EAST COAST

Phuket's east coast has not seen the substantial development that the west cost has. This is largely due to there being virtually no beaches; instead there are mainly rocky embankments. The east coast is popular with sailors, however, and all three of Phuket's marinas are situated there. **Yacht Haven Marina** in the far north has few facilities aside from boat moorings, but both the **Boat Lagoon** and **Royal Phuket**

Marina, located virtually next to each other on the central east coast, are huge developments boasting exclusive bars and restaurants and luxury waterfront accommodation.

Laem Panwa

To the southeast of Phuket Town is the **Laem Panwa** peninsula. Accommodation is limited here, although there are some incredibly luxurious developments. It is difficult to reach, so is best-suited to those seeking a very quiet and peaceful resort-based holiday. Although remote, Laem Panwa is nonetheless very beautiful, with numerous palm-tree plantations and spectacular sea views towards clusters of offshore islands.

Phuket's deep-sea port and naval base are situated here, as is the **Phuket Aquarium and Marine Biological Research Centre** (daily 8.30am–4pm; charge; tel: 0 7639

A venomous lionfish at Phuket Aquarium

1128), where there is a walk-through shark tunnel, tropical fish, reefs and a children's touch pool containing starfish and sea cucumbers. Local buses leave for the aquarium from Ranong Road in Phuket Town.

Sailing on the waters around Laem Panwa is a wonderful experience, and can be arranged at the **Phuket Yacht Club** at **Ao Yon**, the only real beach on the east coast. Empty stretches of sand leading to curving headlands make it particularly picturesque. Once you get beyond the headlands the winds quickly pick up, which is what attracts so many sailors, but the beach itself is well sheltered and good for swimming year-round.

The little-known **Khao Khad View Tower** is often deserted because most people head to the easier-to-reach viewpoints on the opposite western coast, but it is a fantastic

Sea Gypsies

Phuket's 500 or so remaining sea gypsies (chao lay) are the island's oldest residents. They were among the first to settle on Phuket, and although a few today survive by selling shells or beads, the majority still make a very basic living from fishing. Classing themselves as neither Buddhist nor Muslim, they instead worship sea spirits and come from a culture steeped in legend and folklore. One legend holds that a sea gypsy woman once turned into a sea turtle, and as such, the animals are revered as sacred. Once a year, however, it is permitted to hunt and eat turtle meat, while regarding ancient rites. Their dead are delivered to 'dead islands', where their spirits are believed to live on.

Living is simple, and in addition to fish, rice and fruit, the sea gypsies regularly eat worms, lice and other insects. The sea gypsies are nomadic; none own their land, and their heritage has been passed down through the generations. Very few can write, and there are no written records of their past.

Sea gypsy children

point from which to capture some truly spectacular photographs. A two-level viewing tower sits at the highest point of a steep set of stairs, but the 360-degree views from the top make the climb well worth it. Photo maps highlight the sights below, and there are wonderful views out to sea. Parts of Phuket Town, Ao Chalong and the distant outline of Ko Phi Phi are also visible.

Ko Sireh

The tiny island of **Ko Sireh** is separated from Phuket's mainland by a bridge measuring just a few metres. Predominantly home to a community of sea gypsies *(chao lay)*, the area is poor in terms of material wealth but rich in cultural appeal. Be sure to ask permission if taking photographs.

There is a small beach on the eastern side of Ko Sireh, known as **Hat Teum Suk**. It is not really a swimming beach, however, and is visited mostly by Thai families.

THE ISLAND'S INTERIOR

Phuket's interior is a mixture of developed areas of houses, businesses and busy roads, and jungle-filled national parks. The northern town of Thalang is home to some superb temples, whilst Kathu in the south has some good golf courses.

Thalang

Once the administrative centre of Phuket, **Thalang** rapidly lost its prominence with the emergence of Phuket Town, situated around 12km (7 miles) to its south. Thalang has a somewhat shabby appearance, but it holds much historic significance, and there are a number of attractions.

A large roundabout known as the **Heroines' Monument** serves as the gateway to the Thalang district. At the centre of this roundabout are the statues of ladies Chan and Mook, the two heroines who successfully defended Phuket against the

The Legend of Wat Phra Thong

A young boy and his buffalo are said to have suddenly and inexplicably died many centuries ago, when the animal was tied to a mud-covered spiral jutting up from the ground. When the boy's father went to the site of the catastrophe, he discovered the spiral to be the tip of a Buddha image. Villagers attempted to dig the statue up, but attracted swarms of wasps as a result. Only the head was revealed, and further attempts at digging met with disaster. A shelter was eventually built around it, and for many years peace returned. When the Burmese invaded Phuket in 1785, however, they too attempted to unearth the valuable gold Buddha, but a plague of ants descended on them, biting many to death. Today the original Buddha head is encased in a much larger, golden head and shoulders to protect it from theft or damage, and to protect people from falling under the spiritual powers and dark ancient spell it is thought to embody.

invading Burmese in 1785. More is revealed about these two women warriors at the **Thalang Museum** (daily 9am–4pm; charge; tel: 0 7631 1426), which houses artefacts, signs, photographs and other information about Phuket's past. A display explains the Burmese invasion in detail, and other exhibits reveal facts about tin mining, the rubber industry and the culture of the sea gypsies.

The half-buried Buddha at Wat Phra Thong

Around 20km (12½ miles) north of Phuket Town is **Wat Phra Thong**, situated just off the main airport road, near the Thalang District Office. This famous temple is steeped in legend concerning the half-buried golden Buddha found within it *(see box, opposite)*. Only visible from the chest up, this striking statue is said to curse all those who attempt to remove it.

Phuket's oldest temple, built around 545 years ago, is also near here. **Wat Phranang Sang**, meaning 'temple built by a queen', contains the world's largest tin Buddha heads, which were discovered hidden inside the stomach of a large Buddha image in 1973 during a ceremony held by the then governor of Phuket. Also within Wat Phrangang Sang are a large reclining Buddha and a set of statues honouring ladies Chan and Mook.

Khao Phra Taew National Park

Located in the northeast of the island, about 4km (2½ miles) east of Thalang, is **Khao Phra Taew National Park**, the site of Phuket's largest expanse of virgin rainforest, an area of 22 sq km (8½ sq miles). The best time to visit is the May to late-October monsoon season, when flowers are in full bloom and greenery is more vibrant. Khao Phra Taew is home to some attractive walks and waterfalls. The most accessible waterfall is **Bang Pae**, a leisurely 20-minute walk from the park's entrance. Most of the walk is flat, but there are a few steep rocks to navigate which can be slippery during the rainy season. The waterfall is a popular rest stop for lunch or a refreshing dip, but is neither tall nor particularly free-flowing unless the island has recently experienced a lot of rain. Should you feel up to the walk, **Tonsai waterfall** lies a further 3km (2 miles) along the same route and is much more striking, although this, too, can cease to flow during the dry season.

Tonsai waterfall

The information centre can arrange guided treks around this rainforest, where a Dr Darr, a German botanist, discovered the exceptionally rare Lang Khao species of palm around 50 years ago. The tree is fan-like in appearance and stands between 3m and 5m (10–16ft) in height. It is found in only one other place, Khao Sok National Park (situated on the mainland a three-hour drive north of Phuket), and without knowing what you are looking for it would be easy to miss. Likewise, tracks and other evidence of nearby animals, which may not be picked up by the inexperienced eye, will be pointed out along the way.

A rescued gibbon

The **Gibbon Rehabilitation Centre** (www.gibbon project.org) is about a 15–20-minute casual stroll from Bang Pae waterfall. The centre operates on a voluntary basis, relying solely on donations and receiving none of the park fees paid by visitors. Many of the gibbons have been rescued from captivity, as a tourist attraction or pet. They are kept in large enclosures, and although they can be seen from a distance, it is not possible to get too close a view of them as they are being prepared for reintroduction to the wild.

Kathu

As a predominantly residential area, the **Kathu** district has little in the way of accommodation and is not within walking distance of the beaches and entertainment facilities. What is does offer, though, are a number of attractions that are easily accessible from Hat Patong, which is just a 5–10-minute drive away over Patong Hill. At the foot of Patong Hill is **Jungle Bungy**, where participants can leap from a crane suspended over woodland towards the calm waters of Kathu Lake directly below. On the hill itself are two go-kart tracks, one on each side of the road. They stay open well into the evening and are floodlit for night visitors.

Kathu waterfall is best visited between June and October, when water levels are at their highest, the forest is at its greenest and flowers are in full bloom. A trail winds around the waterfall, beginning at an outdoor restaurant that serves refreshments and a basic selection of foods. Near the waterfall is **Phuket Cable Ski** (daily 9am–6.30pm; tel: 0 7620 2525), where visitors can try water-skiing or wakeboarding on a pulley system that runs around a large lake. Also set around the lakes of Kathu is the Loch Palm Golf Course, one of Phuket's most popular golfing greens (tel: 0 7632 1929). The Blue Canyon Country Club (tel: 0 7632 8088) is also nearby.

SOUTHERN PHUKET

Southern Phuket offers visitors a quieter getaway than the west coast. There are a number of peaceful beaches, Phuket's most famous temple, Wat Chalong, and some of the best viewpoints and sunset spots on the island.

Chalong

Situated 8km (5 miles) from the centre of Phuket Town is **Ao Chalong**. A popular location with expats, Ao Chalong has a number of local bars and restaurants, but the main attractions for visitors are Chalong's temple and pier. Ao Chalong is the main base for the island's scuba-divers, as demonstrated by the number of dive operators and water-themed bars and restaurants on the road leading to it – names to look out for include the Sailors Rest and The Lighthouse. At the extreme southwest of Ao Chalong is **Hat Laem Ka**, a beach that is suitable for swimming but visited primarily by locals.

Wat Chalong is the best-known and among the largest temples on the island. It is very popular, and fills with visitors brought in by the coach load. Arriving when it is busy can give it a very touristy feel, so it is advisable to visit in the early morning or early evening to avoid the lunchtime and after-noon crowds. Built in 1837 during the reign of King Rama V, Wat Chalong houses the statues of three monks: Luang Pro Chaem, revered for caring for Phuket's people during the 1876 Miners' Rebellion, and Luang Por Chuang and Luang Por Gluam, highly respected monks who were abbots of the temple during later years. More recently, Wat Chalong has become the first temple in southern Thailand to house the Holy Phra Borom Sareerikatat relic, a piece of Buddha's bones flown over from Sri Lanka.

One of Phuket's most impressive viewpoints is **Ko Nak-kerd**, from which the views towards Ao Chalong and the small islands clustered around it reveal a dramatic colour contrast between the turquoise Andaman waters and the dense green island interiors. Fabulous breezes sweep the hill-top. At the peak of the mountain sits a large Buddha.

Wat Chalong

Asian and African mammals, birds and reptiles are on display at **Phuket Zoo** (daily 8.30am–6pm; charge; www.phuketzoo.com). There are daily elephant, monkey and crocodile shows, and visitors have the opportunity to have their photograph taken with adult tigers.

Located on the mountain road between Chalong and Hat Kata is **Kinnaree House**, where shoppers can purchase Thai silks, batik, pearls and silverware. Also within this large complex is a snake farm that features daily cobra shows, as well as a paintball ground, an ATV (all-terrain vehicle) circuit and the Phuket Shooting Range (daily 9am–5pm; tel: 0 7638 1667).

Snake farms

Many different species of snake can be seen in the island's snake farms, which have daily shows and milking demonstrations. Shows are at set times throughout the day, but a 100-baht tip can usually secure a private tour with an opportunity to get up close and personal with some of the non-venomous species.

Rawai

Despite being very scenic, with a cluster of offshore islands facing it and calm waters lapping against the shores year-round, Phuket's most southerly beach, **Hat Rawai**, is destined never to become as popular as the island's other beaches. Waters are shallow and come right up to the sea wall, so although they appear inviting there is no stretch of sand to lie on, and the jumble of water-covered rocks makes swimming impossible. Rawai is famed for its seafood, and a number of vendors line the beach each evening barbecuing fish caught that day. Longtail boats bob in the water, and the atmosphere is one of calmness and tranquillity.

There is a small sea gypsy community to the east of Rawai Beach. Although you may get a few strange looks if you choose to wander around it, if you do so with respect the locals are generally very welcoming. In particular, never take photographs of people without permission.

Treks through the quieter forests and beaches that surround Rawai can be arranged through the **Phuket Riding Club** (tel: 0 7628 8213). The area's only other inland attraction is the **Phuket Seashell Museum** (daily 8am–6pm; charge), which sells and displays shells primarily from Thailand but with a few offerings from across the world. The shop is open to everyone, but a small entrance fee is payable to get into the museum, where some of the shells are unique. Rarities include the world's

On a tour with the Phuket Riding Club

The spectacular sunset at
Laem Promthep

largest golden pearl, weighing approximately 140 carats, and a shell weighing a whopping 250kg (550lb). Over 2,000 varieties of shell and fossil are on display, with the oldest reputedly dating back to 380 million years ago.

Laem Promthep

Although Kata has a number of fantastic sunset spots, no trip to Phuket is complete without a visit to the most famous one of all, located on the southernmost tip of the island at **Laem Promthep**. Hundreds and sometimes thousands of people come here to stand at this cape and watch the setting sun cast its golden light over a tiny island slightly offshore.

Laem Promthep has a small open-air restaurant serving refreshments and Thai food, which is reasonably priced considering that it monopolises the area. Views on leaving the cape are breathtaking, with **Hat Nai Harn** to the front – its many boats bobbing around the Royal Phuket Yacht Club – and a collection of white windmills blowing around on the hills behind. Hat Nai Harn is reached by following the road around **Nong Han Lagoon**, signposted from the foot of the Kata Hills, or from Rawai. It is a firm favourite with expats who live in the south of the island, and because there is only one hotel directly on the beach, it is fairly quiet throughout the year. The **Samnak Song Nai Harn Monastery**, which occupies much of the beachfront land, has spared Hat Nai Harn from excessive development. Fantastic sunsets can be seen from the 800m- (870yd-) long beach. Although there is little to do here in the way of beach activities and motorised water sports, the odd beach bar and restaurant serve refreshments, and a number of small shops sell beach clothing, jewellery and souvenirs. During the summer months the waters are warm and calm, but Hat Nai Harn is often deserted during the monsoon season due to fierce waves and treacherous swimming conditions. Just around the corner from Hat Nai Harn, past the Royal Phuket Yacht Club, is **Ao Sen**, a tiny and picturesque bay that is rarely visited, simply because many visitors are unaware of its existence.

ISLAND-HOPPING

There are dozens of islands in the waters around Phuket. Although some offer tourist accommodation, many are uninhabited, rugged and untouched, but boast beautiful beaches that are well worth visiting for the day.

The most popular of these small islands can be reached easily from the south coast of Phuket, where longtail boats can be hired from Hat Rawai for anything from a few hours to a full day. Prices vary drastically between seasons, but depending on your ability to barter, a boat will usually cost roughly between 1,200 and 2,000 baht for the day. Boat drivers double as

Heading out to a secluded island

tour guides, and the best way to see the islands is often to agree a rate and then leave the choice of exactly where to go up to them. If you have any special requirements, such as the need for a restaurant if you have not brought your own lunch, be sure to tell your driver. Travelling time between the islands is no longer than 30 minutes. Keep in mind that sea breezes create a deceptive coolness and the boats are usually without shade, making it advisable to wear plenty of sunblock.

Ko Hae (Coral Island)

Situated 9km (5½ miles) off the coast of Hat Rawai is **Ko Hae** (Coral Island). Activities such as jet-skiing and banana boats are available from the two adjacent strips of soft sand beach that face mainland Phuket. Waters are clear and calm close to the shore, and become suddenly and dramatically turquoise at about 5m (16ft) out, where the sea floor suddenly dips.

Sunset at Ko Bon

Snorkelling is possible just beyond this point above a wide reef. Vendors line the beachfront selling snacks and refreshments, and sit-down meals can be enjoyed throughout the day at the island's only accommodation, the **Coral Island Resort** *(see page 135)*. The island was actually named after this resort, and not (as most assume) because of the coral in the waters surrounding it. A few seafood restaurants are set back from the beach, but their opening hours vary and they do not always start serving until the afternoon. As there is only one place to sleep, those staying the night will see the island change from a busy beach popular with day trippers to a serene and secluded location with only a handful of overnight visitors.

Ko Bon

The tiny island of **Ko Bon** is a 10–15-minute hop east of Ko Hae. There is no fresh water or electricity here, which has prevented development and helped Ko Bon maintain a natural, rugged appearance. The exclusive Evason Resort and Spa *(see page 135)*, located on mainland Phuket, owns half of Ko Bon for the use of its guests, and this portion of the island is somewhat more pristine. It is possible to walk from one side of the island to the other, but prices for snacks, refreshments and beach-chair rental are extremely high on the resort-owned side in order to deter non-guests from spending too much time there.

The far side, however, which faces away from the mainland, is owned by local Thai businessmen, and while the beach is not as suitable for sunbathing, it is an excellent spot for snorkellers to inspect starfish, sea cucumbers and crabs in the many rock pools. Snorkellers will need to bring their own equipment because there is nowhere to rent masks and fins. There is little on this side other than the open-air Sit Lo Chia Restaurant, which serves Thai dishes and seafood on tables positioned on the rocks, facing out towards the open sea. This deserted spot becomes crowded with tour groups at midday, but if you can time your visit for sometime after 2pm you are likely to be one of only a few people around.

Ko Racha

The most exclusive of Phuket's nearby offshore islands is **Ko Racha**. Situated 20km (12 miles) south of Phuket, Ko Racha can be reached by longtail boat from Hat Rawai or Ao Chalong. There are two parts to the Racha Islands, the uninhabited Ko Racha Noi and the developed Ko Racha Yai.

Ko Racha Yai is home to the five-star resort **The Racha** *(see page 135)*, situated at **Ao Batok** on the northeast coast. Its sea views and vivid blue waters were no doubt the main appeal to developers searching for the perfect offshore site. Guests at this opulent establishment have complimentary speedboat transfers from Phuket. Many day trips to Ao Batok operate during the high season, when the sands can become a bit crowded, but it is nonetheless a stunning location.

Ko Racha Yai is one of Phuket's most popular sites for scuba-divers; many dive operators choose it as their main dive site. **Bungalow Bay Reef**, offshore from Ao Batok, has sloping reefs brimming with soft corals and tropical fish. Visibility is high and currents are mild, making this location suitable for all levels of experience. More experienced divers can explore a wreck submerged in the waters off **Ao Ter** beach at a depth of 23–35m (75–115ft). **Ao Siam** on the northern coast is among Ko Racha's quietest spots, and although it is not as good for diving, snorkelling conditions are excellent. Facilities are limited, and shallow waters close to shore deter boats.

Ko Racha Noi has some equally impressive dive sites, but they are mainly only suitable for advanced divers. A shipwreck lies off the island's southwest coast, and stingrays and reef sharks hover around the northern pinnacle. Waters are deep and currents are strong right around the island.

Taking a tour around Phang Nga Bay

EXCURSIONS FROM PHUKET

Phang Nga Bay

Situated 65km (40 miles) north of Phuket International Airport, **Phang Nga Town**, on the western side of the Malay Peninsula, rests on flat land surrounded by towering rock faces. It maintains a hidden valley-type feel, away from modern-day development.

Aside from a scattering of caves and waterfalls, there is little to do on Phang Nga's mainland, with the exception of a visit to **Tham Phung Chang** (Elephant Belly Cave). The cave was named for its likeness to the shape of an elephant, with the cave representing the elephant's body and two outcrops forming the tusks. A popular fable tells of a wounded elephant thought to have morphed over time into Tham Phung Chang after dying from a fatal wound. The cave is actually a 1,200m (3,937ft) underground river tunnel, which

Legendary James Bond Island

tour groups navigate daily, using first a rubber dinghy, then a bamboo raft and finally on foot.

With more than 40 islands formed from colossal limestone pillars erupting from the water in all directions, the breathtaking **Ao Phang Nga** (Phang Nga Bay) is undoubtedly the main attraction in Phang Nga province. The bay becomes all the more enchanting in the evening, when the moon casts shadows off these towering rocks into midnight-blue waters, creating a dramatic backdrop against the reds, oranges and yellows of the sunset. Phang Nga Bay hides dozens of sea caves, which are best seen by sea canoe. John Gray's Sea Canoe (tel: 0 7625 4505-6) offers a unique '*Hong* by Starlight' trip into the open-aired *hongs* (caves) to watch fireflies appear as the sun sets.

Other popular excursions are those to **Ko Ping Kan** (Leaning Mountain Island) and **Ko Tapu** (Nail Island), collectively referred to as **James Bond Island**, familiar to many due to its dramatic destruction in the closing scenes of the 1974 Bond movie, *The Man with the Golden Gun*. The 20m (66ft) Ko Tapu is basically a limestone pinnacle jutting out of the water, and thousands pose in front of it from the shores of Ko Ping Kan, just 150m (500ft) away, to recreate the famous shot immortalised by Roger Moore as 007.

All trips and tours around Ao Phang Nga stop at the Muslim fishing village of **Ko Panyi**, where about 500 houses are constructed on stilts over the water, sheltered by a huge rock on one side. **Khao Khien** (Writing Hill) is another common stopping point. Here, colourful sketches of people, crocodiles, dolphins and sharks, thought to be in excess of 3,000 years old, cover the rock walls.

Khao Lak

On the west coast of Phang Nga province is the little beach-side resort of **Khao Lak**, which hit the headlines after it was all but destroyed by the December 2004 tsunami. Khao Lak was steadily restored, however, and is once again blessed with a beauty that attracts visitors by the thousands.

The approach into Khao Lak is breathtaking, with a winding mountain road giving way to an expanse of palms lining the beachfront, which blend seamlessly into crystal-clear waters. There are, in fact, six beaches, separated only by rocky outcrops. From north to south they are Bang Sak, Pakarang Cape, Khuk Khak, Bang Niang, Nang Thong and Khao Lak. The official Khao Lak beach is fairly small at just 800m (870yds), and most of the development is around this and the adjacent Bang Niang and Nang Thong beaches. The region is renowned for its water-based activities, with excellent swimming conditions along all beaches, although after the monsoon rains it is advisable to stay near the northern headlands, where underwater currents are less powerful.

A local man, Khao Lak

The hot and humid **Khao Lak–Laem Ru National Park** (daily dusk–dawn; charge) is slightly south of the beaches. Hornbills, monkeys and the occasional Asiatic black bear are all residents of the park, and the views from here across granite boulders towards the beaches are fantastic.

Similan Islands

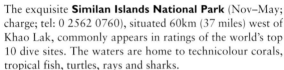

The exquisite **Similan Islands National Park** (Nov–May; charge; tel: 0 2562 0760), situated 60km (37 miles) west of Khao Lak, commonly appears in ratings of the world's top 10 dive sites. The waters are home to technicolour corals, tropical fish, turtles, rays and sharks.

Similan Dive Sites

There are over 30 charted dive sites around the Similan Islands. All have good visibility year-round, with clear waters often reaching 18–25m (60–82ft). During high season this can even reach in excess of 40m (130ft).

Christmas Point (Ko Ba Ngu. No. 9). One of the most visually dramatic dive sites in the Similans, with huge underwater boulders, massive sea fans and some of the most extensive coral growth in the area. Fish are plentiful, with small schools of blue travally, jacks and the odd passing shark.

Fantasy Reef (Ko Similan. No. 8). Underwater rock formations dominate this site, a popular resting spot for clownfish and cowtail rays. Depths range from 15 to 40m (50–130ft), usually with fantastic visibility.

Elephant Head (Ko Similan. No. 8). This site attracts a collection of some of the ocean's most striking inhabitants, from yellow goat fish, snappers, coral trout and lion fish, to reef sharks and the occasional turtle. There are dazzling swim-throughs the deeper you go, and intriguing topography with numerous penetrable holes.

East of Eden (Ko Payoo. No. 6). This is an inspiring site with a concentration of marine life unparalleled elsewhere on the east coast. Among the rarer species are pink frogfish.

One of the beautiful Similan Islands

The nine granite islands of the Similans are covered in varying degrees of jungle, washed by clear ocean waters and scattered with powdery white sand. Each island has a Thai name and a corresponding number from north to south, in descending order. Ko Ba Ngu (No. 9) is located at the northern end of the island chain, followed by Ko Similan (No. 8), Ko Hin Pousar (No. 7), Ko Payoo (No. 6), Ko Ha (No.5), Ko Miang (No. 4), Ko Pahyan (No. 3), Ko Pahyang (No. 2) and Ko Hu Yong (No. 1).

With the exception of Ko Ba Ngu and Ko Miang, the islands are uninhabited. National park status was awarded in 1982, and development was prohibited. Fishing was banned in 1987, and mooring boundaries were established to protect the coral reefs and marine life. The only overnight land accommodation is on Ko Miang, where the national park operates 25 air-conditioned bungalows. Offshore, there are many dive sites *(see box, opposite)*.

Krabi

Kids in Krabi Town

On the mainland, the province of **Krabi**, to the east of Phuket, spans a whopping 4,708 sq km (1,818 sq miles), and is thought to have once existed solely underwater, having evolved into land after the continual flooding and subsiding of sea water created towering limestone peaks where flat plains once dominated. The limestone karsts of Krabi have taken centre stage in commercials, television programmes and movies, including the 2004 blockbuster *Around the World in 80 Days*. More than 130 islands, many of which are tiny or uninhabited, lie in the waters off the coast of Krabi. The best-known islands are Ko Phi Phi and Ko Lanta.

Of the handful of beaches on mainland Krabi, by far the most popular is **Ao Nang**, which might be pretty if it were not for the longtail boats congesting its front. Ao Nang is nevertheless popular for its laid-back atmosphere, and is the main access point for boat trips to the beautiful Laem Phra Nang peninsula.

Laem Phra Nang (Hat Railay)

Backed by towering limestone cliffs on three sides, **Laem Phra Nang** (also known as Hat Railay) is one of southern Thailand's most captivating locations. It is situated a mere 15-minute, 60-baht longtail boat ride away from Ao Nang. This eye-catching peninsula comprises four beaches, each blessed with crystal waters, powder-white sand and limestone cliffs covered with stalactites dripping into the waters below. This also makes Hat Railay one of the world's leading rock-climbing destinations.

The main beaches are **Hat Railay East** and **Hat Railay West**, which are joined by a footpath leading through the island's forested interior. (It only takes around five minutes to get from one side to the other.) While Hat Railay West has a perfect strip of fine white sand and clear, warm waters, Hat Railay East is backed by dense mangrove forest and its shoreline is hampered by jagged rocks.

The immensely extravagant **Rayavadee Resort** is among the most expensive accommodation in all of Thailand, and is the only occupant of **Hat Tham Phra Nang**. Towering limestone cliffs, a completely private location and a beach that embodies the utopian idea of paradise were no doubt the deciding factors when the resort chose this location. Perfection comes at a price, but if your budget does not quite extend to a stay at the Rayavadee Resort, you can still walk to Hat Tham Phra Nang from elsewhere on the Railay Peninsula.

Separated slightly from the rest of the peninsula by a rocky headland, **Hat Ton Sai** emits a greater party vibe than the other beaches, with bungalow-style accommo-

Prow of a traditional Thai craft

Scaling the cliffs of Hat Railay

dation and sea-facing bars offering cheap drinks, cheap meals, and starlit fire-eating and flame-throwing performances, against a backdrop of reggae music and painted neon signs. Full-moon parties occur monthly. This small bay offers amazing views of the open sea, broken in the foreground by a cluster of rocky karsts.

Many of the 650 or so rock-climbing routes that have been marked across Krabi's cliffs are situated around Hat Railay. Views are awe-inspiring, taking in mainland Krabi and extending far out to sea. Experienced climbing guides are available across Railay, but are predominantly located at Hat Ton Sai.

Ko Phi Phi

Ko Phi Phi is roughly equidistant from both Phuket and mainland Krabi. Ko Phi Phi Don and Ko Phi Phi Ley are the largest islands in the archipelago; the remaining four, Ko Bida Nok, Ko Bida Noi, Ko Yung (Mosquito Island) and Ko Mai Phai (Bamboo Island), are essentially just limestone formations projecting from the water's surface.

Ko Phi Phi Don is the main island. **Ton Sai Village**, located at the heart of the island's isthmus, has no roads or cars but is a labyrinth of shops, bars and eateries. Ao Ton Sai lies to the south, and Ao Lo Dalum to the north. **Ao Ton Sai** has a split personality, with a chilled daytime persona that becomes wild and energetic with the setting sun. Thousands flock to evening fire shows, beach bars and clubs, including the island's largest nightspot, The Reggae Bar – an open-air complex with five long bars, an open-roof dance floor, and a Thai boxing ring where kickboxing fights are staged nightly.

Blessed with a stunning natural setting, **Ao Lo Dalum** is encapsulated within palm-covered rock formations wrapping around each side. A sporadic scattering of limestone projections jut from the facing water, and waves rarely roll to shore with anything greater than a gentle lap. Ao Ton Sai is a five-minute stroll away along a footpath marked with a large banyan tree, at the island's narrowest part.

Most accommodation is clustered around these two beach-fringed bays. For some spectacular panoramic sea views, climb up to the viewpoint between the two bays at a height of 186m (610ft).

The view towards Ao Lo Dalum and Ao Ton Sai

Ao Maya, the main location for the film *The Beach*

Around the corner from Ao Lo Dalum and inaccessible by land is **Monkey Bay**. The troops of monkeys that occupy the shores are used to human visitors, and arriving with a few bananas can secure a friend for life – or at least for as long as it takes to get a good photo.

The quietest and most exclusive of Phi Phi's beaches, **Hat Laem Tong**, is located at the northernmost tip of the island. It faces **Ko Pai** (Bamboo Island) and **Ko Yung** (Mosquito Island), both of which offer excellent snorkelling and windsurfing conditions, with flat, calm waters and consistent winds.

Hat Yao (Long Beach) has powder-white sands and captivating views towards Ko Phi Phi Ley. The snorkelling here, above coral, is some of the best on the island. At **Hin Bida** (Shark Point), around 200m (650ft) from the shore, schools of black reef-tip sharks gather in the greatest number in the mornings and evenings.

Ko Phi Phi Ley

Covering just 6.5 sq km (2½ sq miles) in area, the uninhabited **Ko Phi Phi Ley** is located 4km (2 miles) from the larger Ko Phi Phi Don, and is encircled almost entirely by steep pinnacles, which provided much of the backdrop for the film *The Beach*. The breathtaking **Ao Maya** (Maya Bay) was the film's main location. Sheltered on three sides by 100m- (330ft-) tall rock faces, it hides several small beaches, some of which are so tiny that they are only revealed at low tide. Opposite Ao Maya on the western coast is **Ao Pi Leh**, which like Ao Maya is characterised by dramatic vertical cliffs.

The **Viking Cave** is fabled as the one-time stopping-off point for smugglers and pirates seeking shelter from the rough monsoon season. Although some dispute the claim, ancient paintings on the rock walls of Arabian and European sailboats, Viking ships and Chinese junks do seem to imply past visitors of some sort. The most notable attraction today is its abundance of swallows' nests, which are harvested annually by locals, who scale the walls on spindly bamboo ladders. The nests are exported to China as the main ingredient in the controversial delicacy bird's nest soup.

The Beach

Ko Phi Phi was catapulted to fame at the turn of the millennium following the success of the movie *The Beach*, based on Alex Garland's best-selling novel of the same name. The film hit cinemas in March 2000, with Leonardo DiCaprio playing Richard, a backpacker who turns his back on society to live in a hidden lagoon on an undiscovered Thai island. Ao Maya (Maya Bay), on Ko Phi Phi Ley, was chosen as this dream location, and it captivated thousands of those who saw it. Although the filmmakers provoked criticism for allegedly altering the landscape, the main criticism today is that the movie promoted excessive tourism on the island.

Islanders riding through Ko Lanta

Ko Lanta

Ko Lanta Yai (referred to as Ko Lanta) is the largest of an archipelago of more than 50 islands. It is 27km (17 miles) in length and 12km (7 miles) in width. The sea gypsies were among the first settlers on the island, and they initially named it Pulao Satak, which translates as 'island with the long beach'. True to its name, the nine beaches that span the west coast do give the appearance of one giant stretch of sand. All beaches along this coast witness heaven-sent sunsets, and are the location of virtually all of the island's facilities. The eastern side of the island retains a much more rugged image – worth exploring if you fancy getting off the beaten track.

Sunsets along all of Ko Lanta's west-coast beaches are spectacular, but a hilly backdrop and lines of coconut palms make the far northern beaches of **Hat Khlong Dao** and **Ao Pra-Ae** particularly picturesque. One of the island's best snorkelling spots is **Hat Khlong Khong**, where low tide exposes small fish that gather around the rocky underlay of the seabed. Hat Khlong Khong has a distinctive backpacker vibe, with basic bungalows, beach bars and evening fire shows.

The adjacent central beaches of **Hat Khlong Nin** and the smaller, more secluded **Hat Khlong Hin** appear to exist almost independently of the rest of the island – perhaps because access is via a slight detour from the main road. At the start of Hat Khlong Nin is the Rasta Baby Bar, an atmospheric reggae bar displaying the obligatory red, green and yellow rasta flags and filled with scattered floor cushions. This is the first of a number of similar bamboo bars, which span the length of the beach.

The Pimalai Resort and Spa, Ko Lanta's first five-star resort, dominates the 900m (980yd) stretch of sand at **Ao Kantiang**. This quiet bay is marked by golden sand, calm waters and steep cliffs jutting out to the sides. There are only a few other small developments on Ao Kantiang, with the Same Same but Different restaurant at the southern end attracting the most visitors.

A cluster of undeveloped bays sits at the end of a series of dusty dirt tracks to the island's south. **Ao Khlong Chak**, measuring just 400m (440yds), embodies tranquillity, with no accommodation, no noise and often not even another person. The even more remote **Ao Mai Phai** (Bamboo Bay) is yet more isolated, and combines deep waters ideal for swimming with shallow

A boy fills up his hot-air balloon on Ko Lanta

Lanta's lantern

At the southernmost tip of Mu Koh Lanta Marine National Park is a viewpoint on which rests a small white lighthouse. Framed by both sea and mountain, and facing Koh Rok and Ko Phi Phi Ley, this lighthouse has come to stand as Koh Lanta's island symbol and makes for an excellent photo opportunity.

rock pools at the northerly edge, which are more suited to snorkelling.

Encompassing the southern tip of Ko Lanta, and an additional 15 small surrounding islands, **Mu Koh Lanta Marine National Park** became Thailand's 62nd official national park in 1990. Two beaches here fall within the national park, **Laem Tanode** and the rugged **Hat Hin Ngam**, where the park headquarters is situated. A 2.5km (1½-mile) cliff trail originates from here – keep an eye out for fruit bats, wild deer and reptiles, including monitor lizards and snakes.

Snorkelling and Scuba-Diving

Ko Lanta is the access point for one of Thailand's best snorkelling sites – the brightly coloured square-kilometre coral reef of **Ko Rok**. Nearby are the twin peaks of **Hin Daeng** (Red Rock) and **Hin Muang** (Purple Rock), where whale shark sightings are among the highest in the world. These two pinnacles are smothered with red, pink and purple corals, and water temperatures are perfect for the 100-plus types of tropical reef fish that have been catalogued. Other dive sites accessible from Ko Lanta include Hin Bida, Ko Waen and the *King Cruiser* wreck, a car ferry that sunk without fatalities in 1997 (see page 86).

Inland Attractions

An elevated hillside spot known simply as **The Viewpoint** is a magical place to see the sun rise. Head to the blissfully silent Khao Yai Restaurant, surrounded by nothing but trees. Picture-perfect scenes are unveiled as the sun peeks above the horizon, transforming the sky from pitch-black to varying shades of indigo and blue, and casting haunting shadows off the limestone pinnacles rising majestically from the depths of the waters below. Hawks and eagles float freely alongside the restaurant's bamboo platform, seemingly staring out to sea along with you.

To the southeast of the island, at the end of a winding road leading past rice paddies, prawn farms and fields full of grazing wild buffalo is **Lanta Old Town**, home to Chinese merchants, native Thai fishing families, and a small community of Ko Lanta's remaining indigenous people at a 500-year-old sea gypsy village. Modest shop-houses and shacks on stilts at the water's edge make a stark contrast with the luxurious resorts of the west coast.

Off for a dive

WHAT TO DO

Phuket boasts a wide range of indoor and outdoor activities to suit all ages. Be sure to check in advance for details of festivals at your time of travel. Many are extravagant, unique and well worth witnessing.

SPORTS AND OUTDOOR PURSUITS

The main attractions of Thailand's largest island are its sandy beaches and sapphire water. Many visitors are content to take part in no physical activity beyond the flipping of book pages and basking in the sun, but Phuket has more to offer than relaxation and a guaranteed tan.

Boats, jet skis and surfboards can be hired along the main beaches, where rides on banana boats and rubber rings can also be arranged. Hat Patong is the best place to head for jet skis and parasailing. Surfboards and windsurfers can also be hired there, although they are more popular around the headlands of Hat Kata, where the Quiksilver surfing competition takes place each September.

Ko Phi Phi, Ko Lanta and Krabi are all only a few hours away from Phuket, and a number of smaller islands to the south of Phuket can be visited by longtail boat on a day trip.

For a rush of adrenalin – not to mention the thrill of your life – Jungle Bungy at the base of Patong Hill offers the chance to leap from a crane suspended over a large lake. Also on Patong Hill are two go-kart tracks, which are open daily and are equipped with floodlights to enable night rides. There are ATV (all-terrain vehicle) circuits, paintball, a shooting gallery and snake shows at various locations around the island.

Snorkelling in the clear waters off Ko Rok

Water Activities

Game fishing. A relatively recent activity in Phuket, game fishing is increasing in popularity due to the numbers of fish being caught in the deeper offshore waters. Tour agents or private companies will arrange fishing trips. One of the longest-established operators is Wahoo (tel: 0 7628 1510, www.wahoo.ws), which offers some of the best day trips and charters. Aloha Tours (tel: 0 7638 1220) takes visitors to prime locations to catch barracuda, giant trevally and the occasional king mackerel or tiger shark further out to sea.

Sailing. Private and group charters, as well as guided day trips, can be arranged through Sunsail Phuket (tel: 0 7623 9057). For something a little different, any tour agent is able to arrange a trip on the *June Bahtra* Chinese junk, which sails regularly on sunset trips towards Phang Nga Bay.

Safety by the Sea

Phuket's waters are generally very calm, and it is usually only outside the high season that they become choppy. Lifeguards patrol the main beaches, and the internationally recognised coloured-flag system is always in use – a red flag means do not swim, regardless of how the sea looks. Particularly during monsoon season, surface waters that appear calm can mask strong underwater currents; around a dozen tourists drown each year. Do not risk becoming a statistic – if you see a red flag, do not go in the water. Should you become caught in a rip, do not try to fight it. Swim parallel to the beach until you are out of the rip and can make your way back to shore safely.

White Europeans are at high risk of sunburn. In fact, just 10 minutes on a Phuket beach is comparable to around an hour on a scorching day in Europe. Sea breezes and high humidity mask the sun's full power, making heatstroke, sunstroke and severe sunburn common. Use a higher-factor sunblock than you think you need, and avoid the midday sun.

Volleyball on Patong Beach

Phuket is firmly established on the worldwide sailing scene. The Phuket Raceweek regatta (www.phuketraceweek.com) is hosted each July at Rawai and features international yachts from all classes. It is free to watch, or even compete in, with many yachts advertising for crew members in the weeks leading up to it. The more extravagant King's Cup Regatta (www.kingscup.com) at Nai Harn Beach is held during the first week of December in honour of King Bhumibol's birthday.

Sea canoeing. Sea canoeing is extremely popular around the hidden coves of Phang Nga Bay to the north of Phuket. Trips are suitable for most ages and no experience is necessary. John Gray's Sea Canoe is the original and arguably the best operator (tel: 0 7625 4505-6, www.johngray-seacanoe.com). Canoes come with guides, and depart later in the day than other canoe groups in order to avoid the crowds.

Scuba-diving. There are dive centres all over the island. The majority have multilingual instructors who offer first-time

Wreck dive

The *King Cruiser*, a 3,000-tonne car ferry, veered off course on 4 May 1997, hitting the Anemone Reef, 32km (20 miles) off the coast of Phuket, and sinking to the ocean floor within an hour. No lives were lost. Scuba-divers can visit the wreck from Ko Lanta.

explorer dives, as well as PADI (Professional Association of Diving Instructors) certification. Courses involve classroom theory and practical training in both a swimming pool and open water.

Most operators journey to Ko Racha, a 40-minute boat trip offshore, where there are 10 dive sites, featuring large coral reefs, dramatic underwater walls and a 27m- (88ft-) long shipwreck. Ko Racha attracts manta ray, barracuda and huge numbers of large and small tropical fish. Seahorses and leopard sharks are commonly seen at Ko Dok Mai, an hour to the east of Phuket. The Similan Islands, which are frequently listed in the world's top 10 dive sites, can be reached on day trips or longer, live-aboard excursions.

Snorkelling. The waters around Phuket attract fish, crabs, starfish and other marine life, ranging from vivid orange clownfish to giant barracuda, stingrays and reef sharks, but there's no need to scuba-dive to see colourful sea creatures. Snorkelling is especially good around the headlands of Hat Kata Yai and Hat Kata Noi, and inexpensive day trips to the nearby islands can be arranged from mainland Phuket. Most hotels will rent snorkel equipment, and there are numerous dive shops and independent rental booths along the beaches.

Water-skiing and wakeboarding. Situated in the central Kathu district, Phuket Cable Ski (tel: 0 7620 2525; http://phuketcableski.com) is built around a 410m- (450yd-) long and 110m- (360ft-) wide freshwater lake that uses a pulley system to guide participants around the course.

Land-Based Activities

Golf. The exclusive 18-hole, par-71 course at Laguna Phuket Golf Club (tel: 0 7627 0991-2), which was voted 'best golf course in Thailand' by readers of *Asian Golf Monthly* magazine, is set between the sea and mountains, and snakes around lagoons and coconut groves. Also popular are Loch Palm Golf Club (tel: 0 7632 1929), which is set around the largest lake of any course in Phuket, and Blue Canyon Country Club (tel: 0 7632 8088), which boasts two award-winning 18-hole championship golf courses, as well as an on-site spa. Golf clubs can be hired from all courses, and green fees always include golf carts and personal caddy service.

Horse-riding. There are two horse-riding schools on Phuket. The Phuket Laguna Riding School (tel: 0 7632 4199) is located in Bang Tao, and has many horses suitable for younger riders. Phuket Riding Club (tel: 0 7628 8213) is

Preparing for parasailing

further south in Rawai. The club offers treks through forest and along a quiet beachfront. Early morning and late afternoon are generally the best times to ride in order to avoid the hottest part of the day.

Muay Thai (Thai kickboxing). There are camps across Phuket offering training in this sport, ranging from one-off lessons to extensive training over a period of time. Spectators can see fights at 8pm every Monday, Thursday and Saturday at the Boxing Stadium at the far end of Soi Bangla, Hat Patong. Be prepared to see some serious punches thrown, often coupled with injuries and even bloodshed.

Praying before the fight in Patong's Muay Thai stadium

Other Activities

Spas. Small street-side shophouses offering traditional Thai massage and foot reflexology, as well as many luxurious spas, are situated across the island. Thai massage usually lasts one hour; you remain dressed throughout in a loose shirt and trousers that will have been provided. Foot reflexologists apply pressure to specific points on the sole of the foot, which correspond with the internal organs or body parts. A skilled therapist should be able to tell which areas of the body are under stress, simply from exploring your foot. Body and Mind Day Spa offers massages, reflexology,

scrubs, wraps and facials.
They have branches in Hat
Karon, Hat Patong and at
the Boat Lagoon on Phuket's
east coast. Only two spas on
Phuket offer 'Hot Stone Massage', in which hot, mineral-
rich rocks with supposed
therapeutic properties are ap-
plied during a deep tissue

massage to relieve knots and tension. Contact JW Marriott's
Mandara Spa (tel: 0 7633 8000) or the Six Senses Spa at the
Evason Resort (tel: 0 7638 1010) to make a booking.

SHOPPING

Antiques. Rare pieces can be found in shops across the
island, with prices ranging from a few hundred to a few million baht. Most shops specialise in Thai artefacts, but some
of them stock rarities from all over Asia. Look out for Ming
vases from China, Vietnamese lacquerware, and silver from
China and Pakistan. Be aware that Buddha images require
an export permit to be taken out of the country.

Art. Phuket is full of talented artists who spend all day doing
nothing but copying famous masterpieces, designing their
own abstract wall hangings and producing paintings and
portraits based on photographs handed to them by customers. For reproduction art, head to Phrachanukhro Road
in Hat Patong, where a number of galleries are situated
alongside each other. Original works of art are more expensive, but emerging artists frequently hold exhibitions. Check
local newspapers for details.

CDs and DVDs. Although illegal, stalls selling pirated
music and movies are all over the island. Quality varies,

although discs can usually be tested before they are purchased. Buy at your own discretion.

Copied designer items. Clothing, handbags and watches are among the most frequently copied items in the tourist markets. Some goods are obviously fake; others are surprisingly well reproduced. Always haggle from the original asking price.

Fashion. Clothing and accessories are found throughout the department stores, but nowhere is cheaper than the local clothing markets. EXPO Market, in Phuket Town, on Tilok Utit 2 Road, is one of the better ones, and bargains can always be found at the weekend night market, where jewellery often sells for as little as 20 baht.

Food. Fresh and dried chillies and spices, smooth mounds of *kapi* (crushed shrimp paste) and curry pastes prepared before your eyes can all be purchased at the fresh food market on Ranong Road in Phuket Town. Arrive early for the freshest tropical fruits and vegetables.

Gems. Gem stores stock jade from Myanmar (Burma), gold from India and Sri Lanka, and have sapphires and rubies from mines within Thailand. Be prepared to haggle.

Souvenirs. Beads, jewellery, watches, clothes – the list of possible souvenirs is endless. For your best bet head to either of the main shopping centres, Jungceylon in Hat Patong or Central Festival near Phuket Town, or just stroll around the beach stalls and hunt for some unique bargains. There is a French-owned boutique within Siam Indigo Exotique Bar and Restaurant on Phang Nga Road, Phuket Town, which has some unique items of clothing, jewellery and accessories and is well worth checking out.

Tailor-made clothes. Phuket is full of tailors offering quick and inexpensive made-to-measure outfits. A reduction will usually be given for larger orders, and prices can almost always be negotiated. Thai silk is extremely popular, but materials can also be selected from the rolls of cotton, wool and linen stacked from floor to ceiling. Tailors all have clothing catalogues to provide inspiration, and are happy to copy clothes from items or pictures.

Thai silk and fabrics. Ban Boran Textiles in Phuket Town stocks unique fabrics from six Asian countries, and many of the materials can only be found in the villages where they are produced. Most famous for Thai silk, however, is the Jim Thompson empire, of which there are several outlets in Phuket. Materials are usually bought by the metre, although some items may be off the rack.

Colourful printed fabrics

ENTERTAINMENT AND NIGHTLIFE

Bars and Clubs

Phuket Town has come into its own over the past few years with the introduction of more bars and clubs. It is becoming increasingly popular with foreign residents and places little emphasis on the sex trade. For the real action, though, Hat Patong still has the largest, loudest and greatest range of nightlife. The focus in Patong is mainly on cheap drinks, happy hours and booming music, but elsewhere on Phuket there are quiet, classy wine bars and casual sunset bars facing the beaches. Live jazz is performed nightly at Ratri Jazztaurant on Kata Hill, and Joe's Downstairs, situated just north of Hat Patong, is a small but classy bar decorated in pure white, with open-air tables jutting over the rocky seafront. Phuket seems to be unofficially exempt from Thailand's 2001 Social Order Campaign, which states that all entertainment venues must close by 1–2am. Many clubs in Patong, especially, do not even seem to get busy until this time, and the large, open-air Safari Club and Disco on Patong Hill is frequently still in full swing when the sun comes up.

The Go-Go Scene

Soi Bangla is Hat Patong's central street and the hub of Phuket's red-light district. Although extremely blatant, the sex trade is not at all intimidating, and if not taken too seriously Soi Bangla can be surprisingly fun. Although prostitution is illegal, virtually all girls working in the bars and clubs make no secret of the fact that they are for sale. Women

Katoey at Simon Cabaret in Patong

are as welcome as men, though, and should you simply wish to sit with a drink and watch the world pass by, you could do so without being overly hassled. The biggest potential threat, in fact, is to be the man who wakes in the morning to find that the girl he paid for the night before is in fact a *kat-oey* (lady boy), tales of which are extremely common. There are touristy sex shows in some of the more hidden bars, although these have been toned down in recent years. *Kat-oey* dress to impress in extravagant jewelled outfits and feather boas as they parade the street and dance on poles to entice customers into their bars.

Be upstanding

It is customary in cinemas throughout Thailand that prior to the showing of a film, the king's portrait will appear on screen while the national anthem plays. All cinemagoers are expected to stand in silence as a mark of respect.

Cinema

Cinemas can be found inside the Central Festival and Jungceylon shopping centres. As well as standard seats, there are reclining sofa seats and a separate 'first-class cinema', where the ticket price includes drinks and snacks in a welcome lounge, and a huge reclining comfy chair.

CHILDREN'S PHUKET

Tour companies can advise on trips especially suited to children, and many of the larger hotels have excellent on-site kids' clubs. These clubs can usually be taken advantage of by non-guests for a small fee.

The award-winning **Phuket Fantasea** (daily Fri–Wed 5.30–11.30pm, show time 9pm; tel: 0 7638 5333; www. phuket-fantasea.com) is a 57-hectare (140-acre) complex at

Fun in the sun

Kamala that advertises itself as a night-time cultural theme park. There are opportunities for photographs of loved ones riding elephants or holding tiger cubs. The nightly show combines acrobatics, pyrotechnics, illusions and performing animals.

Dino Park (daily 10am–10pm; charge; tel: 0 7633 0625; www.dinopark.com), on the hill between Kata and Karon beaches, is prehistorically themed, with stone tables, draping vines, and staff dressed in Flintstones costumes. Golfers on the mini-golf course pass bellowing dinosaurs breathing smoke from their nostrils.

Siam Safari (tel: 0 7628 0116) and **Island Safari** (tel: 0 7625 4501-3) offer enjoyable and educational sightseeing tours, incorporating elephant- and ox-riding, monkey shows and demonstrations of rubber-tapping and coconut-milking.

The **Phuket Aquarium and Marine Biological Research Centre** (daily 8.30am–4pm; charge; tel: 0 7639 1128) is home to a number of marine species found in the waters surrounding Phuket. Sharks, rays and tropical fish can all be seen without getting wet and there is a touch pool featuring starfish and sea cucumbers.

There are snake farms in several locations on Phuket – children often find these intriguing. Keep an eye out for Phuket Town's **Crocodile and Tiger World**, to open in late 2008.

Calendar of Events

Dates of some festivals and events may vary slightly from year to year, as many correspond to the position of the sun or moon.

February Full Moon: Maka Puja. Candlelit commemorations around temples nationwide mark the meeting at which Buddha preached the doctrines of Buddhism.

13 April: Turtle release festival. Mai Khao and Nai Yang Beaches mark the release of baby turtles into the sea with a grand ceremony.

13–15 April: Songkran (Thai New Year). Nationwide water festival with a party atmosphere throughout the streets. Traditionally there is a big water fight, partly to symbolise washing away the old year and starting the new one afresh, but also simply to enjoy yourself and have fun. Everyone takes part. Expect to get wet.

13–15 May: Loy Rua. Sea gypsy festival to mark the beginning and end of the monsoon season. Offerings for the gods are placed inside model boats and cast away to remove bad luck.

May Full Moon: Visakha Puja. The holiest of Buddhist ceremonies, commemorating the birth, enlightenment and death of Buddha.

July Full Moon: Asanha Puja. Celebration of Buddha's first sermon.

12 August: Queen's Birthday.

September: Quiksilver surfing competition, staged at Hat Kata.

Mid–late October: Vegetarian Festival. Week-long purifying festival testing devotion to the gods. Followers wear white, abstain from meat, alcohol, drugs and sex, and enter trances before piercing themselves with knives and spears.

1 November: Patong Carnival. Festival to mark the beginning of high season, with parades and contests.

November Full Moon: Loy Krathong. Handcrafted floral baskets are filled with candles and incense and floated across seas, rivers and lakes at moonlight to wash away sins and bring good luck.

1st week December: Phuket King's Cup Regatta. Week-long regatta at Nai Harn Beach, featuring yachts from around the world.

5 December: King's Birthday.

EATING OUT

Thai cuisine is known globally for its fragrant aromas, delicately blended spices and fiery chilli kick. Those with a more delicate palate should not worry, however, as there are just as many Thai dishes without the added level of fire as there are with it. Should you unintentionally overdose on the chillies, take a tip from the locals and do not try to cool your mouth down with iced water, no matter how tempted you may be. Instead, reach for a mouthful of plain, steamed rice, which will neutralise the heat almost instantly. Most Thai dishes are quick and simple to make, and often contain just a few key ingredients, which when correctly combined create the illusion of a lot more.

The careful selection and delicate preparation of fresh ingredients is central to Thai cuisine, and although chopping and slicing vegetables, and grinding fresh herbs and spices into pastes for soups, curries and stir-fries can be time-consuming, for the Thai chef this process is simply a part of a time-honoured tradition. An early morning stroll through the fresh food markets of Phuket will show just how important an act the selection of ingredients is. A visit to the markets is typically the first part of the many Thai cookery courses offered on the island.

The heavier, richer and often spicier cooking style native to the Muslim-dominated provinces of southern Thailand has found its way

Sunday buffets

Sunday buffets are a feature of Phuket, with many hotels offering an all-you-can-eat option. Two that stand out from the others are the Twin Palms buffet, famous for its chocolate fountain, and Indigo Pearl Champagne Sundays, which has free-flow champagne included in the price. Make a booking a few days in advance to ensure a table.

Beachside dining at Patong

to Phuket, although true southern Thai dishes, such as the very hot, deep-orange, chilli- and turmeric-based *gaeng choo chee pla* (sour fish soup), are usually found only in remote local restaurants, or at food courts within large shopping centres.

Southern Thai curries are pungent and aromatic, often relying on dried and roasted spices. Best-known is *massaman*, a thick, sweet curry prepared in a peanut base and combined with meat (most commonly chicken), potatoes and often either peanuts or cashew nuts. While other curries are served with rice, massaman is sometimes served with roti, a fried pastry-like bread. Other traditional Thai curries are a lot lighter, prepared in a base of fresh coconut milk, delicate herbs and roots, and flavoured with certain blends of spices. The exception to this rule is *penang*, a curry similar to massaman for its peanut base and creamy consistency, but which is more spicy than sweet and usually only contains meat, with no added vegetables or nuts. Most restaurants adapt their dishes, toning down the level of heat so as not to overwhelm the delicate Western palate. Unless you order an obviously spicy dish or specifically ask for chilli, the level of heat is not usually overpowering.

Aside from traditional Thai food, Phuket has innumerable international restaurants featuring cuisine from across the globe. From budget eateries to celebrity-endorsed restaurants, it is hard not to find something to suit any culinary desire.

Culinary Customs

There is a noticeable irony in the way in which Thai people, who as a nation are naturally slender, appear to spend most of their days eating. Eating in Thailand is a lifestyle in itself, with late-night restaurants, and street vendors serving dishes such as *satay gai* (chicken satay) and *kway teow naam moo* (pork noodle soup), ensuring that there is something to eat at any given hour. The minimal cost of eating out means that few Thais cook at home, and many Thai houses do not even have a kitchen. Eating is a ritual, and food is rarely consumed 'on the go', but rather savoured and enjoyed with friends. Ordering one meal per person is not the norm; instead, a selection of dishes is placed in the centre of the table for the group to share. Unlike the Chinese and

A sea gypsy woman pounding chillies

Japanese, meals are not eaten with chopsticks, but with a fork and spoon. Virtually all dishes, including soups and Thai salads, are eaten with steamed rice, and there will often be an accompanying plate of raw green vegetables, such as cucumber, runner beans and maybe even raw cabbage at the centre of the table to add to your meal. Food courts and street vendors, in particular, have a whole host of accompaniments to go with your meal, from vegetables to raw garlic and chillies, as well as a variety of sauces.

Cookery courses

Thai cookery courses run from a half-day to a full weekend. Most begin with a visit to a local market to select fresh foods, followed by a guided demonstration on how to prepare and cook some of the more common dishes.

Salt and pepper are not used to flavour Thai dishes; expect instead to see a selection of dipping sauces. Spring rolls, barbecued chicken and *goong sarong* (deep-fried prawns wrapped in vermicelli noodle) are accompanied with sweet chilli sauce, although some restaurants also offer sweet plum sauce as an alternative. Fried rice comes with a small bowl of *naam prik pla* (fish sauce with chopped raw chilli), and when ordering fried noodles you will often get a few bowls containing fresh chillies in vinegar, dried chilli, fish sauce and sugar. A sauce that is very popular with rice or noodles, and sometimes served with barbecued fish or meat dishes, is *naam prik phao*, which is a mixture of chillies, shallots, garlic and dried shrimp, roasted and then stir-fried with palm sugar, fish sauce and salt.

Sunday brunch at the Indigo Pearl Resort

What to Eat
Appetisers
Som tam is a refreshing yet spicy salad comprising shredded green papaya and carrot, fresh garlic and chillies, dried prawns and chopped peanuts. It may sound like a strange combination, but it is well worth trying. Thai salads are extremely popular, full of flavour and surprisingly refreshing. If *som tam* sounds a little too adventurous, look for *yam talay* (spicy seafood salad) or *laab moo* (minced pork salad). Alternatively, there is the classic *po pia tod* (spring rolls) or *tod man pla* (Thai fish cakes) – both are served with a selection of sweet sauces.

Soup
Thai soups can be served as an appetiser, or as a main meal if accompanied with rice. *Tom yam* is a thin broth flavoured with chillies, lemongrass, kaffir lime and galangal,

a root similar in taste to ginger. *Tom yam* varies in heat from mild to blazing hot, depending on how much chilli is used. The similar sounding *tom kha* omits the chilli and uses a base of coconut milk for a softer, sweeter taste. Both soups are traditionally served with a choice of seafood, whole prawns or chicken.

Rice and Noodles

Rice is served with most Thai dishes. Most commonly it is simply steamed and served as an accompaniment to a main meal, but the popular fried rice, *kao pad* (which has the interesting pronunciation 'cow pat'), is often a meal in itself. It can be ordered with chicken, pork, seafood or just vegetables, and, like many Thai dishes, comes with a cucumber, spring onion and lime garnish. *Pad thai* is a dry noodle dish stir-fried with bean sprouts, vegetables, meat and spices, and sprinkled with dried chilli and peanuts. Also popular is *kway teow raa naa*, a combination of long, flat noodles stir-fried with vegetables, meat or seafood and soy sauce.

Rice, Rice, Everywhere

The Thais were the first to discover rice cultivation, and Thailand is the world's largest exporter of rice today. Rice is to the Thais what potatoes are to the Irish – a staple food of everyday life. As a minimum, virtually all Thai dishes will come with a portion of steamed white rice. Alternatively, fried rice (*kao pad*) is a meal in itself and comes with a choice of meats, seafoods, vegetables and seasonings. Pineapple-baked rice (*kao obb sapparot*) has a definite 'wow' factor – the meal is encased in an entire pineapple and often accompanied with curried meat, seafood and cashew nuts. Sticky rice can be enjoyed both savoury-style, with fried, seasoned chicken, or sweet, with mango and sweetened coconut milk.

Seafood

Pla muek tod kra tiem prik thai (fried squid with garlic and pepper) is particularly popular. *Pla ka pong neaung manow* translates as steamed whole fish with lemon, garlic and chilli, and *nor mai fa rung phad goong* is fried asparagus with shrimp. For something a little different, *hor mok talay* is steamed spicy seafood wrapped in a banana-leaf parcel.

Chicken and Meat

To order the popular green curry with chicken, ask for *gaeng keow wan gai*. *Gai phad med ma muang* (stir-fried chicken with cashew nuts) is equally popular. *See krong moo tod kra tiem prik thai* is deep-fried pork rib with garlic and pepper.

Sweets

A visit to Thailand would not be complete without sampling the delicious *kao noew ma-muang* (sticky rice and mango). This refreshing but very filling dessert combines fresh chopped mango sprinkled with sesame seeds served over a bed of glutinous sticky rice which has been sweetened with sugar and coconut milk.

Seafood Galore

Phuket has seafood restaurants on just about every street corner. Crabs, mussels, prawns, squid, red and white snapper and even shark are just a few of the specialities found in most restaurants. The unique 'Phuket lobster', which is recognisable by its large size, looks overwhelming, but you may still wish to tackle it, especially since the price of this delicacy is much lower than lobster in the Western world. Many restaurants allow their customers to select their own fish and seafood, and offer a variety of cooking options, including barbecuing, steaming or frying.

Super-fresh seafood is widely available

Fruit

Thais love fruit. It is commonly served for breakfast, with lunch or after dinner, and is always available fresh from vendors along the beachfront, around town and in the markets. Perhaps the most intriguing Thai fruit is the durian – large, green and covered in blunt spikes. Durian is often smelt before it is seen, and is banned in many hotels due to its pungent scent, which has been compared to rotten cheese, sweaty feet and even dead bodies. It tends to polarise opinion – most people either love or hate it. Mangosteens are a small purple fruit and *ngor* (rambutans) are red with soft spikes and a centre similar to a lychee. More familiar are pineapple, watermelon, papaya, mango, coconut and banana.

What to Drink

Water, or *naam*, is essential to keep hydrated in the Thai heat. Tap water is not suitable for drinking, but bottled water is cheap and freely available. Avoid ice that comes in shavings, bits or large chunks, as it may not be fresh, but circular ice cubes with a hole through the centre are safe to drink. These are the kind that are used in the majority of hotels and restaurants.

Fruit shakes are freshly made and sold virtually everywhere. Among the most popular are banana shakes, and the less filling and arguably more refreshing watermelon or pineapple shake. Alternatively, coconut water is full of electrolytes, which can help with rehydration after a spell in the sun.

Phuket Beer is manufactured but rarely seen. Other local beers include Chang, Singha and Tiger, and a few places around the island stock Beer Lao. Heineken is also common, and is the best-known international brand available. All are sold in bottles rather than draught, except in a few of the larger, international pubs and bars. Some of the Irish bars serve Guinness, although it is usually more expensive than most other drinks.

Service with a smile

Cocktails are popular, and most bars have extensive lists, although the quality and taste can vary dramatically from one outlet to another. For visual effect, order one of the cocktails served in a whole pineapple which are available mainly along the open-air bars by the beaches. Local whiskies are inexpensive, popular and a lot more potent than they taste. Brands such as Mekhong and Sang Som are served with coke and ice, or in a bucket with a mixture of Coke and Red Bull – guaranteed to keep you awake for hours.

An exotic cocktail

Wine in Thailand is subject to heavy import charges and is more expensive than beer or spirits. Leave the duty-free spirits on the shelves – they are cheaper to buy once in the country – and instead bring a bottle of wine.

To Help You Order...

Do you have ...?	**Mee ... mai?**
I eat only vegetarian food.	**Chan kin jeh.**
Not spicy.	**Mai phet.**
I can eat spicy food.	**Chan kin phet dai.**
The bill, please.	**Kep taang duay.**
Could we have a table?	**Kor toh dai mai?**
I'd like a/an/some ...	**Khaw ...**

beer	**bia**	ice	**naam khaen**
cup	**thuay**	iced coffee	**kaa-fae yen**
fork	**sawm**	iced tea	**chaa yen**
fruit	**phon-la-mai**	menu	**meh-noo**
glass	**kaew**	spoon	**chawn**
hot coffee	**kaa-fae rawn**	steamed rice	**khao suay**
hot tea	**chaa rawn**	water	**naam**

...and Read the Menu

gaeng keow wan gai	green curry with chicken
gaeng phed gai/neua	red curry with chicken/beef
gai pad bai ka-phrao	chicken stir-fried with hot chillies
gai pad khing	chicken stir-fried with ginger and mild chillies
gai pad med ma muang himaphaan	chicken stir-fried with dried chillies and cashews
gai thawt	fried chicken
gai yaang	grilled chicken
khai dao	fried egg
khai jiaw	Thai-style omelette
kao pad gai/moo	fried rice with chicken/pork
kao tom moo/goong	rice soup with pork/prawns
kluay thawt	batter-fried bananas
kway teow pad see-yu	stir-fried rice noodles
goong phao	grilled prawns
moo krawp	crisp-fried pork
moo yaang	grilled pork
naam kluay pan	banana shake
naam taeng-moh pan	watermelon shake
pad phak	stir-fried vegetables
pad phak buay leng	stir-fried Chinese spinach
pad phak bung fai daeng	water spinach stir-fried with chillies, garlic and soy sauce
pad thai	rice noodles stir-fried with tofu, bean sprouts, egg, dried shrimp
prik naam pla	chillies in fish sauce
som tam	spicy green papaya salad
tom kha gai	galangal and coconut soup with chicken
tom yam goong	spicy lemongrass soup and prawns
yam pla duk foo	spicy catfish salad
yam pla muek	spicy squid salad

HANDY TRAVEL TIPS

An A–Z Summary of Practical Information

A

ACCOMMODATION

The type of budget, backpacker-type accommodation found elsewhere in Thailand is not so evident in Phuket. There are a few youth hostels and some small guesthouses, but these are typically confined to the town centre. Most of the accommodation along the beaches is in hotels, ranging from moderately priced to luxury and even exclusive villas.

As a rule of thumb, accommodation in the south of the island is cheaper than elsewhere, as it receives fewer tourists. There are a couple of high-end resorts, but much of the accommodation is pretty basic and is located above or next to bars or dive shops. It is often comfortable and sufficient if only intended for use as a base, but do not expect any frills. The north of the island, by contrast, is turning increasingly upmarket, with luxurious spa resorts and private villas for rent. The most popular beaches of Patong, Karon and Kata on the west coast are more central, and accommodation here generally falls between the two price extremes.

Rates vary dramatically between high season and low season. Phuket is at its maximum capacity around Christmas and New Year, and despite this being when hotel prices soar, it is also when finding a room can be difficult. Most hotel rooms are reserved for up to six months before this peak period, making advance bookings extremely advisable. Check for hidden costs if staying on the island on Christmas Eve, New Year's Eve, and over the Chinese New Year,

single room	**hawng diaw**
double room	**hawng khoo**
I'd like a single/double room with bathroom.	**Tawng-kaan hawng diaw/ khoo hawng naam nai tua.**
What's the rate per night?	**Khaa hawng thao rai?**

as virtually all hotels, and many guesthouses, hold compulsory 'gala' dinners, for which each guest must purchase a ticket, regardless of whether they attend or not. Some external booking agents neglect to mention this at the time of booking.

Booking agents themselves often publish significantly variable rates, as some receive better allocations and promotional deals for certain hotels than others. Always check for offers on advance bookings, and on stays of more than a few nights.

The majority of hotels charge 10 percent service charge and 7 percent VAT on top of the room rate. Make sure of the total cost at the time of booking, as these charges are often not included in the published price.

AIRPORT

Phuket's International Airport (HKT; tel: 0 7632 7230) is small but generally well operated, and is not as chaotic as might be expected.

Some airlines offer direct international flights from the UK, Continental Europe, Australia and Asia, but most flights stop first in Bangkok, where a number of airlines operate reasonably priced daily domestic flights to Phuket, these include:

Thai Airways www.thaiair.com
Nok Air www.nokair.com
Bangkok Air www.bangkokair.com
Thai Air Asia www.airasia.com

With the exception of Thai Airways flights, which mainly depart from Suvarnabhumi Airport, all other domestic flights from Bangkok operate from the older Dong Muang Airport. Travel time between the two airports varies depending on Bangkok's notoriously congested traffic conditions, but it is advisable to allow at least an hour to get from one to the other.

Flight time from Bangkok to Phuket is approximately one hour and 10 minutes. Expect long queues if clearing immigration in Phuket during peak seasons. There are few shops and restaurants

I need a taxi.	**Tawng-kaan rot taek-see.**
How much is it to…?	**Bai… thao rai?**
Does this bus go to…?	**Rot meh nee bai… mai?**

in the arrival hall, but porters, transport services, hotel desks and tourist information facilities are plentiful.

Air-conditioned taxis are available (the fare to Patong is about 700 baht), and although they may seem more expensive than the few hundred baht charged per person for the airport minibus, they reach the hotels a lot quicker, as there is no waiting around for other passengers to be dropped off at locations around the island first.

B

BICYCLE AND MOTORCYCLE HIRE

Cycling is not common in Phuket, as most people feel safer on the roads in either a car or motorcycle. There are, however, a number of viewpoints that can be cycled around, and tour operators should also be able to advise on areas away from the main roads. If you wish to cycle, contact your hotel reception or a tour operator for details. Motorcycles can be rented at hotels, restaurants, guesthouses, bars and travel agents across the island.

BUDGETING FOR YOUR TRIP

Phuket is inexpensive compared with most Western destinations, but it is slightly more expensive than elsewhere in Thailand. It is realistically possible to eat well on around 500 baht per day, although depending on your preferences you could also get by on a lot less. There are approximately 60 baht to the pound and 30 baht to the US dollar.

Transport: Taxi or tuk-tuk 200–600 baht per trip. Motorcycle taxi 50–200 baht per trip. Average fare of a domestic one-way flight:

2,500 baht. Average fare of a domestic bus ticket to other provinces (air-conditioned bus): 500 baht.

Meals: Dining within even the cheaper hotels is generally a lot more expensive than eating at the local restaurants. On average, breakfast and lunch will cost around 150–250 baht at restaurants, and double this within hotels. Expect to pay 200–500 baht for a reasonable dinner. Dining at the island's top restaurants is more expensive, although still cheap by Western standards, with dishes prepared by internationally renowned chefs costing between 600 and 1,000 baht. While soft drinks, spirits and beer are cheap, wine in Thailand is expensive because of high import duties.

C

CAMPING

Camping is permitted on certain beaches within Sirinat National Park in the northwest of Phuket. Tents can be rented from the visitor centre on the southern end of Mai Khao Beach, and there are a few basic bungalows on Nai Yang Beach. Contact the National Park Authority for details (tel: 0 7632 7407).

CAR HIRE

Rental prices for a standard car range from around 1,500 to 2,500 baht per day (and can be more in peak season). Motorcycles are a lot cheaper; a 125cc bike can be hired for as little as 200 baht for the whole day. Be sure to double-check insurance details, as many of the less reputable companies do not have adequate cover. Lack of insurance, along with failure to wear a helmet, are the most common reasons for intervention from traffic police, who generally impose a 500-baht fine. Although the better-known companies are more expensive, they are also generally more reliable.

Avis tel: 0 7635 1244, www.avisthailand.com
Budget tel: 0 7620 5396, www.budget.co.th

> I'd like to rent a car tomorrow for one day/week with full insurance.
>
> **Yak ja chao rot yon wan phrung nee neung wan/neung aathit phrawm prakan rot.**

When hiring a vehicle, always opt for the full insurance package, especially the Collision Damage Waiver (CDW). Although some credit card companies cover this, you would have to produce an enormous amount of paperwork, which would be difficult and costly to translate from Thai.

CLIMATE

Phuket's tropical climate means that the weather is warm year-round. Even in 'winter' the temperature rarely drops much below 25°C (77°F). The best time to visit is between November and February, when humidity is low, it seldom rains, and the skies are sunny. March and April are usually still dry, but heat and humidity rise in the build-up to the May-to-late-October rainy season. The rainy season is often somewhat misunderstood, as despite the odd cluster of days where driving wind and rain prevail, the skies are generally clear, with heavy downpours only in the evening and at night. Seas at this time can be quite rough, and red flags signalling dangerous swimming conditions should be taken notice of.

Temperatures in the mid- to late 30s (95–100°F) are not uncommon in the March-to-April hot season, although air-conditioned buildings and sea breezes make this time of year more bearable here than in the capital, Bangkok.

CLOTHING

Loose, cotton clothing is preferable for Phuket's tropical climate, although a lightweight sweater might be advisable in the evenings outside the hot season. Street-side stalls sell light plastic rain jackets year-round, which are particularly recommended if riding a motorcycle during the wet season. As the primary religion is Buddhism, it is courteous to cover up in restaurants and shops, and knees and shoulders should be covered if entering temples. Formal attire is practically unheard of in Phuket, and even most businesspeople dress casually. Restaurants and nightclubs are informal, with no standard dress code.

CRIME AND SAFETY

Beware of pickpockets in crowded market places and packed bars. Use common sense – do not tempt bandits by flaunting jewels or belongings. If there is a safe in your hotel room it is advisable to use it. Alternatively, many hotel receptions have an area in which valuables can be deposited; always obtain a receipt.

Violence will not be tolerated in the same manner as in many Western countries, and aggression is frowned upon. Be wary of becoming involved in bar fights, which could lead to a night in jail or a hefty bribe to avoid one.

Drug use and the possession of drugs are taken very seriously in Thailand. The maximum penalty is life imprisonment or death.

Call the police!	**Khaw jaeng tam-ruat!**
Help!	**Chuay duay!**
Call a doctor!	**Khaw riak maw!**
Danger!	**Antaraai!**

CUSTOMS AND ENTRY REQUIREMENTS

For a visit not exceeding 30 days, visitors from many countries, including the UK and US, do not need a visa to enter Thailand, but must have a passport valid for at least six months, as well as a return or onward ticket. Visas can usually be extended by up to 10 days at the immigration office in Phuket Town. For stays of more than a month, obtain a 60-day visa at a Thai consulate or embassy in your own country before you travel. For details, see www.thaivisa.com or the websites of Thailand's Immigration Bureau (www.immigration.go.th) and the Ministry of Foreign Affairs (www.mfa.go.th).

Currency restrictions. There is no restriction on the import of foreign currency, but amounts over the equivalent of US$10,000 must be declared. On leaving the country, you may take out up to US$10,000 or the equivalent in foreign currency (more if declared on arrival).

Export of antiquities. When leaving Thailand, note that the export of any images of Buddha or other deities is prohibited. The export of antiquities without special permission from the Fine Arts Department is also prohibited. Some shops will be able to obtain the necessary permits for you, or you can contact the office directly: National Museum, Fine Arts Department, 4 Na Phra That Road, Bangkok, tel: 0 2224 1370.

D

DRIVING

Road conditions. Although not busy and congested like Bangkok, conditions on Phuket are still nothing short of chaotic. Most motorists show little regard for other drivers, or even for themselves. It is very rare that a car will willingly give way to you. The flashing of headlights by an oncoming vehicle means that it is coming through regardless. The best way to drive is to assume that everyone that can get in your way, will – that way there are fewer surprises. Do not be shocked to see vehicles driving on the wrong side of the road, or families of four or five balanced on one motorcycle.

Although it is illegal, drink-driving is commonplace, and there are regular road accidents. Statistically, there is at least one fatal crash each week, with the majority involving motorcyclists.

Rules and regulations. An international driver's licence is required for visitors to Thailand. The official speed limit is 50km/h (30mph) in towns, 80km/h (50mph) on main roads and 90km/h (56mph) on highways.

Fuel. Service stations are plentiful, but many shut before 8pm as part of a government initiative to save energy. At many points along the roadside after dark, people sell old whisky bottles filled with fuel, which can be siphoned into your tank should you be running low. While these bottles are fine for motorcycles, they should only be used for cars as a last resort.

Parking. Major shopping centres have covered parking, which gets more cramped at weekends. Parking bays are situated along most streets. In many cases, which side of the road you are permitted to park on will be determined by whether the date is an odd or even number. Look to signs for an indication.

If you need help. Telephone the agency from which you rented the car to come and help you. In an emergency dial the tourist police (tel: 1155).

Road signs. Major roads are signposted in English. Beware of contradictory road signs. Often a no U-turn sign will be placed immediately in front of a sign to tell you U-turns are permissible. A blue sign with a white arrow pointing to the left or right at a junction indicates that if conditions are safe you can ignore the traffic lights and turn on the red light.

accident	**u-bat-fi-het**
collision	**rot chon**
fill (the petrol tank)	**dem**
flat tyre	**yang baen**
Help!	**Chuay duay!**
Police!	**Tam ruat!**
Slow down!	**Cha-cha!**

E

ELECTRICITY

The standard current in Thailand is 220-volt, 50-cycle AC; most hotel rooms have an electrical outlet for shavers; some also have 110-volt sockets. Plugs are two-pin, and you'll need adaptors (and transformers, depending on where you're coming from).

EMBASSIES

All embassies are located in Bangkok:
Australia: 37 Satorn Tai Road, tel: 0 2344 6300.
Canada: 990 Rama IV Road, Abdulrahim Place, 15th Floor, tel: 0 2636 0540.
Ireland: 28th Floor, Q.House Lumphini Building, 1 Sathorn Tai road, tel: 0 2677 7500.
New Zealand: All Seasons Place, 87 Wireless Road, tel: 0 2254 2530.
UK: 14 Wireless Road, tel: 0 2305 8333.
US: 120–122 Wireless Road, tel: 0 2205 4000.

Some countries have consular representatives in Phuket. They can be reached on the following numbers:
Finland: tel: 0 7621 5585
France: tel: 0 7628 8828
Germany: tel: 0 7635 4119
Italy: tel: 0 7638 1792

embassy	**sathaan thoot**
passport	**nang seu doen thaang**
visa	**wee-saa**
Where's the British/ American embassy?	**Sathaan thoo angkrit/ amerikaa yoo thee nai?**

Sweden: tel: 0 7632 7006
US: tel: 0 7634 2270

EMERGENCIES

In case of emergency dial 191. For less dire emergencies contact the
tourist police on 1155.

G

GAY AND LESBIAN TRAVELLERS

Due to Thailand's tolerant Buddhist culture, there is little discrim-
ination against gays and lesbians. There are no gay movements
because there is little anti-gay sentiment in the country.

Although the gay scene is not as evident as in Bangkok, there are
several gay-owned establishments in Phuket Town and Patong, including bars, restaurants and small hotels. Most of the action takes place
around the Paradise Complex on Rat Utit Road in Patong, and there
is an annual gay festival (www.gaypatong.com) in February.

Purple Dragon is a highly respected travel company that provides
services for gay and lesbian travelers. More information can be
obtained at www.purpledrag.com.

GETTING TO PHUKET

By air. Most visitors stop off in Bangkok for a few days en route to
Phuket. The island's international airport receives daily non-stop
flights from Europe, Australia, Malaysia, Hong Kong and Singapore.

Domestic flights from Bangkok leave daily from Suvarnabhumi
Airport (Thai Airways) and Don Muang Airport (all other airlines).
By bus. The rise of budget airlines has seen a fall in the demand for
coach travel, but buses leave Bangkok's Southern Bus Terminal
nightly for the 14-hour trip.
By boat. Foot passengers from Krabi and Ko Phi Phi are dropped
at Rassada Pier in Phuket Town. The journey from each place can

take anywhere from two to three hours, depending on the weather and sea conditions. Boats from Ko Lanta travel via Krabi or Ko Phi Phi, although they often do not run between May and October due to bad weather.

GUIDES AND TOURS

A list of licensed English-speaking guides can be obtained from the Tourism Authority of Thailand (TAT). By law these guides are required to wear their official photo identification card around their neck at all times. Rates are not fixed and will vary according to where you would like to go and within what period.

Often a guide will come with a driver, particularly on group tours. Hotel receptions can give an indication of the approximate rates that would be considered reasonable. It is customary to provide lunch or invite the guide to eat with you, particularly on full-day trips. Alternatively, you may tip the guide and driver at the end of the day to cover the cost of lunch.

Rates for organised tours vary, but not enormously, as most tours are arranged through independent operators competing for the same business. Tours can usually be booked at very short notice, and mostly include return hotel transfers.

Guides and tours are plentiful on Phuket and can be arranged at your hotel reception, or at one of the many tour offices located along the beaches and in shopping centres.

H

HEALTH AND MEDICAL CARE

No vaccinations are required to enter Thailand. Anti-malaria tablets are also unnecessary, but during the rainy season you should spray repellent to deter the mosquito that carries dengue fever. Infection is not common, but if you begin to exhibit severe flu-like symptoms, headaches, nausea and vomiting, contact a doctor immediately.

Tap water is not safe to drink. Bottled water is cheap and readily available everywhere. Ice in drinks is generally safe in reputable restaurants. Round ice with a hole through the centre is made from bottled water, but avoid all others, particularly ice shavings.

Over-indulgence in rich or spicy foods, and too much sun, are as common a cause of stomach disorders as actual bugs. Experiment with new foods gradually and avoid becoming dehydrated.

Local health clinics often only take cash, but credit cards are accepted in all major hospitals. Hospitals are of an excellent standard, and there are 24-hour pharmacies across the island. The costs of medical treatment and supplies are significantly lower than in Western countries. Many medications that would usually require prescriptions back home can be dispensed freely over the counter.

a bottle of drinking water	**nam yen nung khuad**
I need a doctor.	**Pom(if male)/chan(if female) tong karn maw.**
I need a dentist.	**Pom/chan tong karn maw fan.**
pharmacy	**raan khaai yaa**
hospital	**rohng phayaabaan**
doctor	**maw**

HOLIDAYS AND FESTIVALS

Holidays and festivals abound in Thailand. Phuket has the additional week-long celebration in mid- to late October to mark the Vegetarian Festival. Participants, who wear only white clothes and abstain from meat, alcohol, onion, garlic, drugs and sex, summon spirits, enter trances and pierce their bodies with implements ranging from chopsticks to palm leaves.

Many Thai holidays are fixed to the lunar calendar, so dates may vary slightly from year to year. Banks and government offices close during holidays, but daily life is not generally disrupted. The exception to this is Thai New Year (Songkran), when most businesses close, although the quieter streets are a lot more noticeable in the capital, Bangkok, than on Phuket.

During religious holidays and government elections, alcohol is often forbidden to be sold in bars, shops and restaurants.

1 January	New Year's Day
6 April	Chakri Day, honouring Rama I
13–15 April	Songkran (Water Festival for Thai New Year)
1 May	Labour Day
5 May	Coronation Day
12 August	Queen's Birthday
23 October	Chulalongkorn Day, honouring Rama V
5 December	King's Birthday and National Day
10 December	Constitution Day
31 December	New Year's Eve

Variable dates:
Chinese New Year (first month of the lunar calendar, usually Jan/Feb).
Maka Puja (full moon in February). Commemoration of meeting at which the Buddha preached the doctrines of Buddhism.
Visakha Puja (full moon in May). Celebrates the birth, enlightenment and death of the Buddha. Most holy Buddhist ceremonial day.
Asanha Puja (full moon in July). Celebrates Buddha's first sermon.
Vegetarian Festival (ninth month of the lunar calendar, usually mid- to late Oct).

L

LANGUAGE

English is widely used across Phuket, but it is useful to know some basic Thai phrases when in restaurants or shops. There are many dialects and sub-dialects, and certain tones of the Thai language in

Phuket are noticeably different from those in Bangkok. The language can be difficult to master, as despite being more basic than English in terms of grammar, it uses intonation to distinguish between identical words. In some cases, one word can have up to five different pronunciations and meanings. There are 44 consonants, plus dozens of vowels, compounds and tone marks.

M

MAPS

Basic but often adequate maps can be picked up free in the arrival hall at the airport, and at hotel desks and tourist information offices. More detailed maps can be found in bookshops. The 'Phuket Day and Night Groovy Map' is one of the best.

MEDIA

The *Bangkok Post* and *The Nation* are Thailand's leading English-language newspapers. They are available at airports, most hotels, shopping centres and branches of 7-Eleven stores. They are also updated daily online and can be read at www.bangkokpost.com and www.nationmultimedia.com.

There are two English-language weekly newspapers on Phuket. They are the *Phuket Gazette* (www.phuketgazette.com) and the *Phuket Post* (www.phuket-post.com). Both can be bought at outlets across the island.

Thailand has five terrestrial television channels, which often show foreign shows, although they will be dubbed into Thai. Leading hotels usually have a selection of satellite TV channels, which usually include CNN and the BBC world news services 24 hours a day.

MONEY

Currency. The unit of currency in Thailand is the baht (abbreviated THB, Bt or B), which is divided into 100 satang. Banknotes come in denominations of 20, 50, 100, 500 and 1,000 baht. Coins are 25 and 50 satang, and 1, 2, 5 and 10 baht.

Banks and exchange facilities. Normally the exchange rate at banks is the most favourable. After the banks are closed you can change money at your hotel, at exchange booths or at shops displaying a sign in English saying 'money changer'.

Banks and money changers in tourist towns will accept virtually any currency.

Credit cards. Major hotels, restaurants and shops are accustomed to the well-known international credit cards. Small eateries and small shops tend to accept cash only.

ATMs. Facilities for using your debit or credit card to withdraw money automatically are widely available on Phuket.

Can I pay with this credit card?	**Jaai pen bat credit yang nee dai mai?**
I want to change some pounds/dollars.	**Yaak ja laek plian pound/dollar.**
Can you cash a travellers' cheque?	**Laek plian chek doen thaang dai mai?**
Where's the nearest bank?	**Thanaakhaan klai-sut yoo thee nai?**
Is there a cash machine near here?	**Mee khreuang atm klai thee nee mai?**

O

OPENING TIMES

Business hours are 8.30am–noon and 1–4.30pm, Monday–Friday. Many offices also open for a half-day on Saturdays. Banks are open 8.30am–3.30pm. Central Festival shopping centre, outside Phuket Town, opens its doors at 9am, although only the food supermarkets are accessible before 11am. Jungceylon, in Patong, opens at 10am. Both shopping complexes close at 10pm.

State-run museums are closed on Monday and Tuesday.

All bars and establishments selling alcohol are required to close by 1am, but Phuket seems to be exempt from the rule, and generally there will always be somewhere to party until the early hours.

P

POLICE

Thai military police are recognisable by their beige uniforms and white helmets with a red stripe. Those based around the tourist areas usually have passable English. Also generally stationed near the beaches are the tourist police, who wear a similar uniform to the military police but with a tourist police patch on the shoulder. The tourist police can be reached by dialing 1155 from any phone in the country. They are generally more helpful in minor situations than the military police.

police	**tam-ruat**
tourist police	**tam-ruat thawng thiaw**
Where's the nearest police station?	**Sathaanee tam-ruat thee klai-sut yoo thee nai?**
I've lost my...	**... haai**
wallet/bag/ passport.	**kra-bao ngoen/kra-bao/ nang seu doen thaang.**

POST OFFICES

Phuket's main post office is located on Montri Road in Phuket Town, with additional branches in Patong, Karon, Rawai and Thalang. Opening hours are 8.30am–4.30pm Monday–Friday and 9am–noon on Saturday.

The cost of sending letters and postcards by airmail is often less than in Western countries. Post should arrive at its destination within a week. Registered mail can be arranged at any post office.

Where's the nearest post office?	**Praisanee klai-sut yoo thee nai?**
express (special delivery)	**EMS**
registered	**long tha-bian**

PUBLIC TRANSPORT

Public transport is plentiful around the tourist areas, beaches and shopping centres, but elsewhere on the island it is notoriously lacking. Taxis and tuk-tuks are significantly more expensive than in the rest of the country.

Local buses. Small, blue public buses *(songthaew)* are very cheap (often no more than 10–30 baht per trip) but are infrequent and painfully slow. All buses go from and to the central bus terminal on Ranong Road in Phuket Town. Services depart half-hourly between 7am and 6pm to the various beaches, but no buses run from one beach to another.

Motorcycle taxis. Although a cheap way to travel, a motorcycle taxi is certainly more risky. They can be convenient for short trips, but are not advisable for longer journeys. High season sees at least one death on average per week from road collisions, the majority involving motorcycles.

Taxis. Taxis in Phuket are not easily distinguishable from normal cars with a driver. In most places, they are few and far between, with the exception of the shopping centres, where taxi ranks display fixed rates for the main beaches. None are metered. They are mostly air-conditioned, and are more comfortable than tuk-tuks.

Tuk-tuks. Unlike their three-wheeled cousins in Bangkok, Phuket tuk-tuks are four-wheeled, bright red and resemble a shrunken minivan. Passengers sit on two wooden benches facing each other in the back. Tuk-tuks are not equipped with meters, and fares must be agreed before climbing aboard. Never agree to the initial asking price, and expect to pay more in bad weather or after midnight. Most drivers speak good English.

boat	**reua**
bus	**rot meh**
taxi	**thaek-see**
Where can I get a taxi?	**Mee rot thaek-see thee nai?**
What's the fare to...?	**Bai... raakhaa thao rai?**
Where is the bus stop?	**Rot meh klai-sut yoo thee nai?**
What time does the next bus to... leave?	**Rot pai... thiaw naa awk kee mohng?**
I want a ticket to...	**Yaak ja seu tua bai...**
single/return	**thiaw diaw/bai klap**
Will you tell me when to get off?	**Khaw bawk wehlaa theung laew?**

R

RELIGION

The majority of Phuket's Thais are Theravada Buddhist, although there is also a large Muslim community. Temples and mosques are found across the island. Many expat residents are Christian, and interestingly, large numbers of Thais are also turning from Buddhism towards Christianity. The violence associated with religion in the south of Thailand has not affected Phuket, and all faiths are generally well tolerated.

Phuket Christian Centre: 74/123 Phunphon Road, Phuket Town, tel: 0 7624 6380, www.phuketchristiancentre.com. Church with English-language services on Sundays at 10.30am and 6.30pm.

Wat Chalong: Bypass road, Chalong, tel: 0 7621 1036. Phuket's most famous Buddhist temple. Open daily.

T

TELEPHONES

Thailand's country code is 66. To make an overseas phone call from Thailand you must first dial 001, followed by the country code and area code. For international call assistance dial 100.

Telephone and fax services are provided at most hotels or at business centres and internet cafés around the island. Rates (usually per minute with a three-minute minimum) are posted in English.

Prepaid international phone cards can be bought at post offices, but public telephones are not always the best option for long-distance calls due to noisy locations or bad connections.

Users of GSM 900 or 1800 mobile phones with an international roaming facility can hook up automatically to the local Thai network. Check with your service provider if you are not sure. Alternatively, Thai SIM cards can be bought for a few hundred baht, with prepaid top-up cards widely available. Mobile phones can be bought second-hand for as little as 2,000 baht.

TIME ZONES

Thailand is seven hours ahead of GMT. Night falls between 6pm and 7pm year-round, so daylight-saving time is not observed.

telephone	**thohrasaap**
long-distance call	**thohrasaap thaan klaai**
international call	**thohrasaap rawaang prateht**
Can you get me this number?	**Khaw mai-lehk thohrasaap nee dai mai?**
reverse-charge (collect) call	**thohrasaap kep plaai thaang**

TIPPING

Tipping is not the norm between Thais, but is common among foreigners. Taxi drivers already charge extortionate rates in comparison with the rest of Thailand, so it is not usual to tip on top of their fare. Hotel maids can be tipped 20 baht per day, or given a lump sum on checkout. Twenty baht is also standard for porters in mid-range hotels. A 10 percent tip is customary in restaurants and for massage therapists.

TOILETS

Toilets in Phuket are generally cleaner than those in Bangkok, although you may still encounter squat toilets in some small restaurants or in local Thai areas, and certainly at bus or service stations if you venture off the island. A helpful tip for women is to face away from the door, in the opposite manner as they would in a Western toilet. Squat toilets are flushed by pouring water from a large bucket or tank with a plastic scoop.

| Where are the toilets? | **Hong nam yu tee nai?** |

TOURIST INFORMATION

The Tourism Authority of Thailand (TAT) operates information stands in the arrival hall at Phuket International Airport.

You can obtain leaflets, maps and advice at the TAT Office: Thalang Road, Phuket Town, open daily 8.30am–4.30pm, tel: 0 7621 2213, www.tourismthailand.org.

Overseas representatives of the Tourism Authority of Thailand can be found in the following countries:

Australia: 75 Pitt Street, Royal Exchange Building, 2nd Floor, Sydney 2000, tel: 61-2-9247 7549.

UK: 98–99 Jermyn Street, London, SWIY 6EE, tel: 020-7925 2511.

US: 611 North Larchmont Boulevard, Los Angeles, CA 90004, tel:

1-323-461 9814; 61 Broadway, suite 2810, New York, NY 10006, tel: 1-212-432 0433.

WEBSITES AND INTERNET CAFÉS

Internet cafés are plentiful in Phuket. Most charge a standard rate of 1–3 baht per minute with a 10-minute minimum charge. Some useful websites include:

www.phuket.com Information guide and booking service for accommodation and tours around Phuket.

www.phuketgazette.com Regularly updated online version of Phuket's leading English-language newspaper.

www.phuket.net Information on all aspects of Phuket, with an online directory of contact details for most Phuket businesses.

www.thaiair.com The site of the state-run airline, Thai Airways International, with timetables, fares and availability details for all flights to Thailand, as well as domestic flights.

www.tourismthailand.org The official site of the Tourism Authority of Thailand, which has plenty of information on all aspects of travel in Thailand.

www.sawasdee.com Detailed information on tourist attractions throughout Thailand, and information and booking service for accommodation and tours.

YOUTH HOSTELS

There are few youth hostels on Phuket, but among the better-known is the Phuket Youth Hostel (www.phukethostel.com), to the south of Phuket Town. For more information about youth hostels on the island, refer to the Hostelling International website, www.hihostels.com.

Recommended Hotels

Hotel prices vary widely across Phuket. Generally, the average hotel standard is more upmarket than elsewhere in Thailand, and the cost of a room is consequently higher than in Bangkok and on the other islands. The north of Phuket in particular has a lot of luxurious villas and upmarket accommodation.

The following price scale is based on mid-season rack rates for a superior room per night, excluding the compulsory 7 percent VAT and 10 percent service charge. Prices can change dramatically from peak to low seasons, and if booking accommodation independently, always ask for discounts – most hotels will give them freely.

Rates are often much cheaper than advertised for stays of three nights or longer, and even similar booking websites can vary greatly in the rates they charge, as some are allotted promotional rates throughout the year by the hotels that favour them.

Prices rise substantially during the peak-season Christmas and New Year period. Most rooms are booked months in advance, so be sure to make a reservation well ahead of time.

$$$$$	over 8,000 baht
$$$$	6,000–8,000 baht
$$$	4,000–6,000 baht
$$	2,000–4,000 baht
$	below 2,000 baht

PATONG

Avantika Boutique Hotel $$$ *41/1 Thaweewong Road, tel: 0 7629 2801-8, fax: 0 7629 2809, www.avantika-phuket.com.* Small and intimate beach-facing hotel with only 31 rooms. Located opposite the beach at the quieter southern end of Patong, but with shops, bars and restaurants only a few minutes' walk away. The central Soi Bangla is approximately 10 minutes' walk away. Rooms are sophisticated in design, with dark woods offset against Thai silk furnishings, and all have ocean views. Swimming pool, spa, bar, restaurant.

Baan Sukhothai $$ *70 Bangla Road, tel: 0 7634 0195-6, fax: 0 7634 0197, www.phuket-baansukhothai.com.* One of the only recommendable hotels directly on Soi Bangla, and surprisingly quiet considering its prime location. The resort is not overly modern, but is spotlessly clean and very friendly, with a large swimming pool. Great option for budget travellers.

Baan Yin Dee $$$$ *7/5 Muean Road, tel: 0 7629 4104-7, fax: 0 7629 4108, www.baanyindee.com.* Truly serene boutique resort with just 21 rooms and suites, all traditionally Thai in design, with dark woods, rattan furniture and white linens. Guest rooms, a terraced restaurant and an opulent four-tiered swimming pool all enjoy elevated sea views from a spectacular mountainside location.

Burasari $$$ *32/1 Ruamjai Road, tel: 0 7629 2929, fax: 0 2678 0102, www.burasari.com.* Upmarket ambience at mid-range prices. The resort, situated on a quiet street set slightly back from the main beach road, has attracted a lot of attention since celebrity chef Keith Floyd opened a restaurant here in 2007. Rooms at the Burasari are positioned around the two central swimming pools, each surrounded by palms and tropical flowers. Shopping and dining amenities are nearby.

Impiana Phuket Cabana $$$ *41 Thaweewong Road, tel: 0 7634 2100, fax: 0 7634 0178, www.impiana.com.* Patong's only true beachfront accommodation. The luxuriously designed beach huts are located directly on the sand and are well spaced to ensure privacy. Facilities within the main building reflect the indulgent nature of the resort, with a high-end spa and the exclusive Sala Bua restaurant, which is again Hat Patong's only true beachfront restaurant.

Stoney Monday Oasis Hotel $ *35/1 Rat Utit Road, tel: 0 7629 0363, fax: 0 7629 0368, www.stoneymonday.com.* Australian-owned budget hotel with clean, spacious rooms and free WiFi for guests. Relaxed and friendly atmosphere, with a ground-floor restaurant, a rooftop garden and very informative staff. Situated around a five-minute walk from the main shopping district, and less than 10 minutes' walk from the beach.

KARON

Andaman Seaview $$ *127/35 Patak Road, tel: 0 7639 8111, fax: 0 7639 8177, www.andamanphuket.com.* Somewhat quirky in appearance, with white Corinthian-style pillars and different-coloured rooms on each of its four floors. This friendly, family-run establishment is an excellent option for those wishing to avoid the carbon-copy type of chain hotel. Hat Karon is directly opposite, and Hat Kata is only a five-minute walk away. All rooms are face the sea, and the 'de luxe pool access' rooms open directly onto a large swimming pool that winds around the hotel.

The Village Resort and Spa $$$ *566/1 Patak Road, tel: 0 7639 8200-5, fax: 0 7639 8206, www.thevillageresortandspa.com.* With only 34 artistic and somewhat eccentric-looking villas, each bearing an uncanny resemblance to the shape of a mushroom, this delightfully unique boutique resort appears hidden among jungle, yet is just opposite the beach. The quiet villas are split between pool view and jungle view, and are incredibly peaceful and romantic.

KATA

Aspasia $$$ *1/3 Laem Sai Road, tel: 0 7633 3033, fax: 0 7633 3035, www.aspasiaphuket.com.* Indulgent, Mediterranean-looking resort with mustard and terracotta walls offset with trailing vines and flowers. Bird's-eye sea views from the resort's elevated hillside position are fantastic. Rooms are modern and incredibly spacious. All have balconies and many have sunken Jacuzzis in the bathrooms. A regular beach shuttle bus is available.

Kata Beach Resort $$ *1 Pakbang Road, tel: 0 7633 0530-4, fax: 0 7633 0128, www.katagroup.com/katabeach.* Blessed with a prime position directly ahead of Kata Beach, this large yet relatively low-rise hotel projects a smaller, more intimate feel than its size would imply. Numerous facilities make it an excellent family choice, although couples will also benefit from an adults-only swimming pool and a romantic, dimly lit sea-facing restaurant.

Mom Tri's Boathouse Hotel $$$ *2/2 Patak Road, tel: 0 7633 0015-7, fax: 0 7633 0561, www.boathousephuket.com.* Very romantic boutique resort, which perfectly combines Western comforts with Eastern style. The peaceful ambience is heightened by the hotel's air of exclusivity, with an emphasis on intimate service and a relaxing and indulgent stay. There is direct beach access, and the sun sets over the sea each evening, which all guest rooms face. Highly recommended for honeymooners.

Sugar Palm Resort $ *20/10 Kata Road, tel: 0 7628 4404, fax: 0 7628 4438, www.sugarpalmphuket.com.* Bright and modern hotel just a few minutes' stroll from Kata Beach and surrounded by a number of restaurants and small cafés. Spotlessly clean rooms are designed in soft cream with an individual accent colour, and all have balconies. A rectangular swimming pool with fountains and water features sits in the centre of this excellent-value hotel, which has frequent offers on room rates.

KAMALA

Aquamarine Resort and Spa $$$ *17/36 Moo 6, tel: 0 7631 0600, fax: 0 7631 0630, www.aquamarineresort.com.* Dramatically perched upon the hilltop, this resort has dazzling sea views from all around, and from each of the Thai-designed rooms. Very peaceful and tranquil due to its elevated position, but no beach access as a result. There is a regular shuttle bus, however, which makes the five-minute trip to nearby Hat Kamala throughout the day.

SURIN

Ayara Hilltops $$$$$ *125 Moo 3, Srisoonthorn Road, tel: 0 7627 1271, fax: 0 7627 1270, www.treetops-arasia.com.* Sea views are spectacular from the 48 villas comprising this striking boutique resort. Private suites are elevated on the mountainside, surrounded by palm trees, vines and flowers, and are well spaced along private walkways. The beach is within easy walking distance, and there is a sea-facing swimming pool. A number of rooms also have private outdoor swimming pools and/or Jacuzzis.

The Chedi Resort and Spa $$$$ *118 Moo 3, Cherngtalay, tel: 0 7632 4017-20, fax: 0 7632 4252, www.ghmhotels.com.* Tropical-looking hotel with individual thatched bungalow- style rooms, each with a terrace or balcony facing the Andaman Sea. Bungalows start directly on the sand, and reach back to the resort's peak, from which views are fantastic, although a lot of walking is required. There is a striking octagonal black-tiled swimming pool, and one of Phuket's most upmarket spas on site.

BANG TAO

Amanpuri $$$$$ *118/1 Moo 3, Srisoonthorn Road, tel: 0 7632 4333, fax: 0 7632 4100, www.amanresorts.com.* Amanpuri is Phuket's most famous retreat, frequented predominantly by the rich and famous. It is unaffordable for many, but should your budget stretch this far you are guaranteed the ultimate in opulence and extravagance, from butler service in private villas to access to a fleet of luxury cruisers, which dock daily at the Amanpuri's private beach.

Banyan Tree Resort and Spa $$$$$ *33 Moo 4, Srisoonthorn Road, tel: 0 7623 4374, fax: 0 7632 4375, www.banyantree.com.* Despite being the most exclusive hotel within the Laguna Phuket group, reasonable prices can often be secured with advance bookings. Rooms have private gardens and a swimming pool, with additional pools and a golf course on site. Awarded 'World's Best Spa Resort' by *Condé Nast Traveller* magazine, and 'Best Resort Hotel in Asia' by *The Asian Wall Street Journal*.

NAI YANG

Indigo Pearl $$$$ *Nai Yang Beach and National Park, tel: 0 7632 7006, fax: 0 7632 7338-9, www.indigo-pearl.com.* Re-branded and refurbished in 2006 from a mid-range to much more exclusive hotel, although some attractive room rates are offered at certain times of year. Popular for its extensive facilities, which compensate for its distance from the main tourist strip. Highly recommended free-flow champagne buffet on Sundays during peak season.

MAI KHAO

JW Marriott $$$$$ *231 Moo 3, Mai Khao, tel: 0 7633 8000, fax: 0 7634 8348, www.jwmarriottphuket.com.* Extremely exclusive, and perfect for those seeking truly to get away from it all, but only recommended for a purely resort-based holiday due to its secluded location at the far north of Phuket. With countless facilities, however, and a breathtaking location as the only hotel on Phuket's longest beach, it could be questioned why you would want to leave the resort in the first place.

PHUKET TOWN

On-On Hotel $ *19 Phang Nga Road, tel: 0 7621 1154.* Made famous by its role as the bustling backpacker resort in the hit movie *The Beach*, this character-filled hotel is undeniably basic, but priced accordingly at just a few hundred baht per night. Not overly comfortable for an extended stay, but an excellent place to meet other travellers and a good base from which to explore Phuket Town.

Royal Phuket City Hotel $$ *154 Phang Nga Road, tel: 0 7623 3333, fax: 0 7623 3335, www.royalphuketcity.com.* Situated in the heart of town, with its own coffee shop and lounge area with piano bar, Phuket Town's largest hotel is also its best. Its size makes it slightly impersonal, but all sights are within walking distance, staff are friendly and rooms are clean and spacious.

LAEM PANWA

Cape Panwa Hotel $$ *27 Moo 8, Sakdidej Road, tel: 0 7639 1123, fax: 0 7639 1177, www.capepanwa.com.* Situated right on the beach, this stunning low-rise hotel is blessed with direct access to unspoilt sands, backed by rows of swaying palms. All rooms at Cape Panwa face the sea, and many of the newer rooms have Jacuzzis and private pools. There are weekly cultural activities, including Thai cooking, Thai language lessons, Batik painting and massage classes.

RAWAI

Evason Phuket Resort $$$$ *100 Viset Road, tel: 0 7638 1010-7 fax: 0 7638 1018, www.sixsenses.com/evason-phuket.* Upmarket resort more suited to couples than families. Boasts a luxurious spa, a number of beautiful sea-facing restaurants, a small stretch of private beach and even its own island for the exclusive use of hotel guests.

NAI HARN

The Royal Phuket Yacht Club $$$$$ *23/3 Moo 1, Viset Road, tel: 0 7638 0200, fax: 0 7628 9016, www.theroyalphuketyachtclub.com.* Favoured by international celebrities, royalty and those with large wallets, this extravagant resort was awarded the prestigious 'Best Leisure Hotel in the World' by *Condé Nast Traveller* magazine, and was voted Best Resort Hotel in Thailand by the World Travel Organisation. It is the only hotel with direct access to Nai Harn Beach, and has all the facilities you would expect of a top-class resort.

KO HAE

Coral Island Resort $$ *48/11 Chaofa Road, Chalong Bay, tel: 0 7628 1060, fax: 0 7638 1957, www.coralislandresort.com.* The only accommodation on Coral Island, making it somewhat more highly priced than hotels of the equivalent standard on the mainland. Provides a comfortable stay, however, with clean, air-conditioned rooms and the only swimming pool on the island. Quiet and very peaceful in the evenings once Phuket's day trippers have left.

KO RACHA

The Racha $$$$ *42/12–13 Moo 5, Rawai, tel: 0 7635 5455, fax: 0 7635 5637, www.theracha.com.* The perfect island getaway, accessible by private speedboat from mainland Phuket. Villas are decorated in elegant white, with garden bathrooms and rain showers. The rooftop infinity pool has uninterrupted sea views, and there is a luxurious spa and restaurant. Wonderful option for couples, but probably not suited to families with young children.

Recommended Restaurants

Phuket can accommodate any palate at any budget. The island is brimming with all sorts of restaurants, ranging from family-run establishments and fast-food joints to very expensive eateries with celebrity owners.

Reservations are only usually necessary in resort restaurants and the more exclusive independent establishments, although bookings are recommended in high season and during public holidays. Credit cards are accepted at most restaurants, but street vendors and some smaller establishments only accept cash.

Not all establishments open for breakfast, but 'lunch' and 'dinner' usually span long hours. Lunch can mean anything from 11am to 3pm, and dinner usually starts at 6pm and doesn't finish until around 10.30am. Many restaurants open at noon and remain open throughout the day.

Drinks do not usually add a significant amount to a bill, other than in high-end establishments. Ordering wine by the bottle, however, can cause a significant jump in the total due to the inflated import charges on wine and champagne throughout Thailand.

The following prices are for a three-course meal, excluding tips and drinks. Tips are discretionary, with 10 percent of the food cost being the norm.

$$$$	over 1,000 baht
$$$	600–1,000 baht
$$	300–600 baht
$	below 300 baht

PATONG

Flavors $$$$ 94 *Thaweewong Road, tel: 0 7629 2576.* Open Monday–Saturday 5pm–midnight. Romantic French-owned and managed restaurant offering an extremely friendly and intimate level of service. Dishes are deliciously innovative, and there is a fine selection of wines from around the world. The supreme of duck with tamarind and ginger Grand Marnier sauce is a restaurant speciality, and for an Asian twist, the traditional French crêpe suzette with coconut milk is particularly recommended.

Floyds $$$$ *18/110 Ruamjai Road, tel: 0 7637 0000.* Open daily for dinner only. Superb quality of food from celebrity chef Keith Floyd. A la carte menu focuses on just 10 or so dishes for each course, but they are exceptional. The cocktail list is fantastic, and the raspberry mojito is sinfully delicious. There is live music nightly in this open-air restaurant, and be sure to keep an eye out for the owner himself, who often pops in for a visit.

Nanai Buffet BBQ and Thai Food $ *155 Nanai Road, tel: 0 7634 5429.* Open daily for dinner only. Popular with both Thais and tourists, 99 baht (US$2) buys unlimited beef, chicken, pork, prawns and squid, all barbecued at your table Korean-style and accompanied by a large selection of vegetables and noodles. Cheap, filling, and a deliciously fun and interactive way to eat.

Sala Bua $$$ *41 Thaweewong Road, tel: 0 7634 2100 ext 8306.* Open daily 11am–midnight. Patong's only true beachfront restaurant was voted one of the best restaurants of 2007 by *Thailand Tatler* magazine. Renowned chef Ronnie Macuja prides himself on his seared beef tenderloin, and the desserts are arguably among the best on the island. Try the Thai sticky rice and mango with an interesting caramel twist.

Savoey Seafood $$ *136 Thaweewong Road, tel: 0 7634 1170.* Open daily for lunch and dinner. Select your meal from freshly caught daily offerings at the front of the restaurant. Try the whole snapper, either barbecued or steamed with a choice of sauces. The fried squid with garlic and pepper is also recommended. Meat dishes are available for those who are not keen on seafood.

KALIM

Baan Rim Pa $$$ *223 Prabaramee Road, tel: 0 7634 0789.* Open daily noon–midnight. Phuket's most exclusive Thai restaurant is perched above a jagged rock face and boasts dramatic views of the sea below. The food here is of unbeatable quality, and is based around the less spicy 'Royal Thai' style of cuisine. A speciality of the house is the *goong sarong* – deep-fried prawns encased in crispy vermicelli noodles, which are freshly prepared and individually wrapped every morning.

Da Maurizio $$$$ *223/2 Prabaramee Road, tel: 0 7634 4079.* Open daily noon–midnight. Oozing romance, this small and secluded restaurant is set atop a cluster of rocks just metres from the foamy fizz of the waves that lap against it. Because there is only a handful of tables, bookings are advisable, and, although the Italian dishes are a little on the expensive side, they are among the best that Phuket has to offer.

KARON

Kashmir Restaurant $$ *316/1–2 Patak Road, tel: 0 7639 6330.* Open daily 11am–midnight. The only authentic Indian restaurant on Karon Beach is Indian-owned and managed. All dishes are of the highest quality and come highly recommended, but the mixed grill and tandoori options are house specialities. A large selection of Thai and Western dishes is also available.

Ruam Thep $ *120/4 Moo 2, Patak Road West.* Open daily for lunch and dinner. Cunningly hidden Thai and seafood restaurant situated on the cosy southern corner of Hat Karon. Service is friendly, and the menu is large enough to justify sipping on one of the popular fresh banana milkshakes as you read through it. Although unassuming in appearance, the food at this little restaurant is fantastic.

Wildfire $$–$$$ *509 Patak Road, tel: 0 7639 6139.* Open daily 8am–1am. This split-level restaurant is particularly enticing from the outside for its fire-lit torches and jungle-like appearance. A la carte international dishes are offered on the top floor, but far more popular is the Brazilian grill on the bottom, where wood-fired pizzas and cocktails served in coconuts can be enjoyed on chunky wooden tables facing the beach.

KATA

Capannina $$ *30/9 Moo 2, Kata Road, tel: 0 7628 4318*. Open daily noon–11pm. Popular restaurant with wood-fired ovens, featuring authentic dishes from across the various regions of Italy. Warm and welcoming mustard and terracotta walls and a mix of open-air tables and covered cushions create a cosy dining atmosphere. Beware of the large pizza – measuring a whopping 60cm (23in) in diameter, it often requires a table of its own.

The Coffee Pot $$ *110/3 Taina Road, tel: 0 7633 3203*. Open daily 8am–10.30pm. Deceptive due to its name, this Australian-managed eatery is less of a coffee shop and more of a meat-lover's paradise. Those in the know travel island-wide for the mammoth home-cooked Sunday roast dinners, but equally as enticing are the huge steaks and seafood barbecued daily on a large street-side grill. If its reputation does not lead you there, then your nose will.

Mom Tri's Boathouse Wine and Grill $$$ *182 Kata Road, tel: 0 7633 0015*. Open daily for lunch and dinner. This romantic beach-facing restaurant is home to one of Phuket's most extensive wine lists and is the winner of numerous wine awards. Choice of air-conditioned indoor tables or alfresco decking just metres from the waves. The ambience is casual yet upmarket, with a menu to match. The rock lobster trilogy with green curry, Armagnac and Thermidor sauces is to die for!

Oyster Bar $$ *Moo 2, Kata Road*. Open daily for breakfast, lunch and dinner. Do not be fooled by the name, for the Oyster Bar does not only serve seafood but also dishes up generous helpings of authentic Thai and Western food all under one roof. The large menu makes it an excellent option for families or for those with different dining desires.

KAMALA

Rockfish $$–$$$ *33/6 Hat Kamala, tel: 0 7627 9732*. Open daily 8am–late. Beautiful elevated cliff-side location with panoramic views out towards the bay. Minimalist tables sit on wooden decking, subtly lit to create a chic and somewhat trendy ambience. The menu is a mix of Thai and Western specialities, with tempting fusion offerings such as chilli-marinated tuna with fresh coconut juice.

SURIN

Catch Beach Club $$$ *Surin Beach Road, Cherngtalay, tel: 0 7631 6567.* Open daily 8am–1am. Alfresco eatery with indoor tables and a long bar, as well as bamboo tables set directly on the sand to create a very elegant and tropical feel. Seafood is the house speciality, with fresh catches offered up daily and a highly recommended Friday night buffet extravaganza. Weekend bookings are advised.

Silk Bar and Restaurant $$$ *The Plaza Surin, 5/50 Moo 3, Cherngtalay, tel: 0 7627 1702, www.silkphuket.com.* Open daily for lunch and dinner. Chic and trendy eatery with food to match at the latest dining venue from Hong Kong's acclaimed Lan Kwai Fong Entertainments group. Silk is ultra-modern, with a cosmopolitan vibe and an air of richness. The predominantly Thai menu features mouth-watering *gaeng phed ped yang* (red curry with roast duck) that goes well with a large glass of good red wine.

BANG TAO

Lakehouse Tropical $$ *Laguna Phuket Entrance, tel: 0 7627 1384.* Open daily for lunch and dinner. Dine by a lake to the sounds of chirping cicadas and soft background music in this romantic tropical restaurant situated just outside the Laguna Phuket complex. Features classic Thai and Oriental barbecue cuisine. The house speciality – a whole roasted piglet – is divine, but must be ordered 24 hours in advance.

The Supper Club $$$ *Unit 20/382 Srisoonthorn Road, tel: 0 7627 0936.* Open daily 6pm–1am. Contemporary international cuisine with mouth-watering meat dishes, including grilled Australian beef tenderloin and herb-coated rack of lamb. Fairly expensive considering the informal atmosphere, but food quality seems to justify the price.

PHUKET TOWN

2 Gusti $$ *74–75 Central Festival, tel: 0 7620 9124.* Open daily for lunch and dinner. Located in the grounds of the Central Festival shopping complex, this quirky new restaurant is based on the interesting concept of Italian and Japanese fusion cuisine, prepared by chefs of each nationality. Try the sushi pasta for something truly unique. A traditional Italian menu is available for the less daring.

Natural Restaurant $ *62/5 Soi Phutorn, tel: 0 7622 4287.* Open daily 10.30am–11.30pm. Submerged between plants and trees, this multi-level Thai restaurant reflects its name, with patrons dining amid a jungle-like interior. All dishes are delicious, but the stir-fried kale with salted fish is particularly worth trying. Excellent location for large groups to gather and enjoy a fabulous meal at very reasonable prices.

Salvatore's $$–$$$ *15–17 Rasada Road, tel: 0 7622 5958.* Open Tuesday–Sunday for lunch and dinner. Voted Thailand's Best Italian Restaurant by *Thailand Tatler* magazine, this is easily one of Phuket's finest authentic Italian restaurants. Food from the à la carte menu is outstanding, and the daily specials are usually exceptional. Particularly recommended is the crab gratin to start – and anything else for the main course!

Siam Indigo Exotique Bar and Restaurant $$ *8 Phang Nga Road, tel: 0 7625 6697.* Open daily Wednesday–Monday for lunch and dinner. This French-owned eatery is one of Phuket Town's best-kept secrets. Located inside an 80-year-old building, Siam Indigo features tall windows and thick-beamed ceilings, and is captivatingly decorated with colourful mosaic-tiled art pieces contrasting with crisp, white furniture. The menu predominantly features exquisite Thai dishes from the freshest ingredients selected that day. Be sure to save space for dessert – the patisserie-style baked selections are outstanding – but for sheer indulgence it is hard to beat the white chocolate mousse.

Tung-Ka Café $$ *Rang Hill, Korsimbee Road, tel: 0 7621 1500.* Open daily 11am–11pm. Perhaps the restaurant with the best view of Phuket Town, Tung-Ka Café is located halfway up the winding Rang Hill, where it has been serving Thai cuisine for over 30 years. Lunchtimes are less busy, but the view in the evening is far more impressive. All dishes are good, and the penang curry is particularly worth trying. Be sure to specify if you want it without excess chillies.

CHALONG

Kan Eang $$ *44/1 Viset Road, tel: 0 7638 1212*. Open daily 10am–10pm. Large yet intimate open-air, pier-side restaurant with tiny fairy lights dotted in the trees and well-spaced wooden tables lit in the evenings by simple candlelight. Peaceful location where small boats bob in the waters as diners tuck into some of the Phuket's most delicious yet well-priced Thai and seafood dishes.

RAWAI/NAI HARN

Chao Khun $$ *39/23 Viset Road*. Open daily for breakfast, lunch and dinner. Extremely popular with expat residents, this swanky restaurant is characterised by deep-red walls, comfortable bamboo furniture and a classy Thai and international menu. Outstanding hotel-quality buffet breakfasts for a bargain 140 baht per person are served daily.

Mama Klong Seafood $ *Rawai Beach Road*. Open daily for lunch and dinner. Dine as the locals do, with a selection of freshly caught and prepared seafood dishes served on thin reed floor mats, scattered on the sand and facing the water's edge. Food is cheap but of guaranteed quality, and is often brought in from the fishing boats just moments before being cooked.

Nikita's $$ *Corner Rawai Beach Road, tel: 0 7628 8703*. Open daily from 9am until late. As the only bar and restaurant directly on Rawai Beach, Nikita's is a beautiful location for a quiet Sunday afternoon. The menu is predominantly Thai, and although there is a strong emphasis on seafood, the meat dishes are equally as tasty. Views are of fishing boats bobbing near the cluster of islands beyond, and the ambience is one of relaxation and tranquillity.

INDEX

Berlitz® pocket guide

Phuket

First Edition 2008
Written by Lauren Smith
Edited by Anna Tyler and John Mapps
Series Editor: Tony Halliday

All Rights Reserved
© 2008 Berlitz Publishing/Apa
Publications GmbH & Co. Verlag KG,
Singapore Branch, Singapore

Printed in Singapore by Insight Print
Services (Pte) Ltd, 38 Joo Koon Road,
Singapore 628990. Tel: (65) 6865-1600.
Fax: (65) 6861-6438

Berlitz Trademark Reg. U.S. Patent Office
and other countries. Marca Registrada

Photography credits
Jon Davison 6; David Henley/CPA 34; Hans
Höfer 15; John W. Ishii 9, 10, 11, 19, 21, 22, 27,
28, 37, 53, 57, 60, 63, 69, 71, 72, 73, 74, 76, 78,
79, 82, 91, 98, 99, 104, 105; Joerg Kohler/Old
Maps & Prints Co. Ltd 13; Ingolf Pompe 75;
Reinhard Schmid/4Corners Images 97; Steve
Van Beek 16, 48; Marcus Wilson Smith 55;
Nikt Wong 8, 17, 18, 24, 29, 31, 32, 36, 39, 40,
42, 44, 46, 47, 49, 50, 51, 56, 59, 61, 62, 64, 67,
68, 81, 85, 87, 88, 92, 94, 100, 103.

Cover picture: Giovanni Simeone/SIME-
4Corners Images

Every effort has been made to provide
accurate information in this publication,
but changes are inevitable. The publisher
cannot be responsible for any resulting
loss, inconvenience or injury.

Contact us

At Berlitz we strive to keep our guides as
accurate and up to date as possible, but if you
find anything that has changed, or if you have
any suggestions on ways to improve this guide,
then we would be delighted to hear from you.

Berlitz Publishing, PO Box 7910,
London SE1 1WE, England.
fax: (44) 20 7403 0290
email: berlitz@apaguide.co.uk
www.berlitzpublishing.com